CYCLES OF POWER:

A User's Guide To The Seven Seasons Of Life

by

PAMELA LEVIN

Health Communications, Inc.
Deerfield Beach, Florida

Pamela Levin
Ukiah, California

Library of Congress Cataloging-in-Publication Data

Levin, Pamela
    Cycles of power: a user's guide to the seven seasons of life/by
Pamela Levin.
        p.   cm.
    Bibliography: p.
    ISBN 0-932194-75-3
    1. Developmental psychology. 2. Adjustment (Psychology) 3. Self-
actualization (Psychology) 4. Life cycle, Human — Psychological
aspects.   I. Title.
BF713.I49 1988   88-7232
155 — dc19   CIP

French translation *Les cycles de l'identite* published by InterEditions, Paris, France, 1986.

© 1988 Pamela Levin
ISBN 0-932194-75-3

Published by Health Communications, Inc.
            Enterprise Center
            3201 Southwest 15th Street
            Deerfield Beach, FL 33442

Cover Design and Illustration by Reta Thomas
Airbrushed Sphere by Ron Williams

C O N T E N T S

Preface v

PART I
Nature's Design For Life 1

Chapter 1   The Cycle 3

Chapter 2   Cycle Sabotage 13

Chapter 3   Seeds Of Power 27

PART II
The Seven Stages Of The Cycle 33

Chapter 1   Stage One:
                  The Power Of Being 35

Chapter 2   Stage Two:
                  The Power Of Doing 51

Chapter 3   Stage Three:
                  The Power Of Thinking 69

Chapter 4   Stage Four:
                  The Power of Identity 87

Chapter 5   Stage Five:
                  The Power Of Being Skillful 105

Chapter 6   Stage Six:
                  The Power Of Regeneration 121

Chapter 7   Stage Seven:
                 The Power Of Recycling 137

                 PART III
                 Developmental Exercises 149

Chapter 1   Creating A Vision 151

Chapter 2   Developmental Script Questionnaire 155

Chapter 3   Using The Think Structure For
                 Creating Your Personal Developmental
                 Affirmations 159

Chapter 4   Exercises For Developing The Power
                 Of Being 163

Chapter 5   Exercises For Developing The Power
                 Of Doing 169

Chapter 6   Exercises For Developing The Power
                 Of Thinking 175

Chapter 7   Exercises For Developing The Power
                 Of Identity 183

Chapter 8   Exercises For Developing The Power
                 Of Being Skillful 189

Chapter 9   Exercises For Developing The Power
                 Of Regeneration 195

Chapter 10   Exercises For Developing The Power
                 Of Recycling 201

Conclusion   207

Glossary   211

Bibliography   215

References   219

PREFACE

We human beings long to discover and integrate ourselves into the promising perfection found in the pounding surf, an exquisite stand of trees, a parade of stars against the moonlit night sky. We search as if seeking a mirror in which to find ourselves. What does it mean to be human? What do we have in common with rocks, trees, ocean, sky, animals, people? What is our relationship to the universe? How are we organized? *Cycles of Power* is a work focused on these queries. It is about both discovery and recovery. It is about finding, reclaiming and learning to be sustained in the basic growth cycle which is our human birthright.

The life course of each individual has a basic cyclic structure through which personal history unfolds stage by stage. These are our growing seasons, our teachable moments, our critical learning periods: phases when given the right conditions, we can make gigantic leaps. To maximize nature's gift, we need only carry out the appropriate developmental tasks. Nature's pattern forms the basic ground for responding to all the other variables of life.

Evolving cyclically means that certain issues and themes return over the course of time as we come back to the beginning point and pass through them again, often in a more sophisticated way. We even remark that someone is acting like a two-year-old or a teenager or a baby. This natural recycling is nature's cleaning schedule — a way of providing regular, scheduled healing periods to flush out old toxins, bring in fresh nutrients and heal old scars.

The architecture of this extra-genetic learning system is one our ancestors knew intuitively. They lived in the natural rhythm of their own lives in the same way they lived in the natural seasons of the year. They understood themselves to be part of nature and nature to be part of them. As modern people we need to relearn that it is both natural and healthy to repeat childhood stages in adulthood.

Many aspects of life are clarified by knowing the stages within the cycle, their essential tasks and how to use them as support to achieve success. For example, the essential emotional nutrients in each stage nurture healthy development within the natural seasons. Because it is natural to grow from birth until death, it is natural to show signs of stress when that growth process is interfered with. Considering how much effort it would take to try to prevent a season of the year from occurring to work against nature's pattern, it becomes easy to understand why we feel stressed and develop physical symptoms. Thus using this view, some otherwise puzzling physical symptoms may be readily translated into missing sequences of development and the process by which they can be completed is made clear (see Part Two).

The information presented here is intended as a guide in harmonizing human life with human nature as part of nature. It is both a map of healthy development and a structure for successfully realizing personal dreams. Its principles apply to recovery from a dysfunctional childhood, to raising children, to being a satisfied parent, to the creation of healthy, growth-affirming relationships, to increasing effectiveness in any aspect of life. We can relax, knowing that we can prevent future crises by carrying out present tasks using methods to deal with them which are implied in our body clues. Finishing growth tasks as they arise, we completely avoid developmental crisis — at midlife, at retirement or any age.

Further, we can return to foundation levels of development to finish incomplete sequences of childhood. It is never too late for any adult to have a happy childhood because limiting decisions can be changed, early issues which bind up energy can be resolved, and developmental gaps from childhood can be filled in with new healthy experiences, providing a firmer foundation that supports more sophisticated adult abilities. Such work is necessary because no parent can be perfect or provide all the love, nurturing and support needed at every age in childhood and no child is able or necessarily ready to take in what is given. Therefore discovering the lack of some inner resources in adulthood is a relatively common experience. However, we need not just make do or avoid what is missing.

Instead, we can take what we were given and expand it to be all of what we need. Results seen as only dimly possible become reality.

The process by which this is accomplished involves a natural ability called regression. Done without conscious knowledge or an appropriate environment, it can be most unfortunate. Being a two-year-old, five-year-old or six-month-old in a grown-up body can be extremely hazardous. A method called corrective parenting provides under contract the same environment and temporary protection necessary to complete what regression attempts to gain — a new organizational experience at the inner level where it is missing. Thus "adult children" heal the inner child to become truly grown up.

The key is to learn to greet grown-up dysfunctions, whether physical or mental, emotional or relational, as messages from the inner child who still needs something and hasn't given up. Accurately translating and appropriately acting on these messages, we can truly liberate ourselves from helplessness in otherwise tyrannizing circumstances.

Cycles of Power is based on nearly two decades of research involving over 1,000 people for a few hours up to a few years. I have been child and parent, the student and "the studied." My aim was to discover common patterns, unifying trends and to communicate commonalities.

I came to this study from a medical background as a nurse who was weary of human suffering and eager to prevent it. Training with psychiatrist Eric Berne, author of *Games People Play* and founder of Transactional Analysis, I began to discover patterns common to certain ages. For example, 26-year-olds often had difficulty concentrating, felt as if the bottom were dropping out of their lives and also had skin problems. Thirty-two-year-olds frequently had trouble with authority and were dissatisfied with a perceived junior standing in the social fabric.

The importance of these discoveries I sensed only vaguely at the time. Later, living in the country I lived and learned nature's ways. Returning to the city to work with clients I finally recognized how the deeply personal is also universal. Within us is the same pattern of organization manifested in every form from the molecule to the Milky Way. Rather than proceeding in a straight line from birth to death, human life follows nature's pattern and that pattern is cyclical.

Even though we each modify it, this generic cycle is universally valid.

This theory has passed many times through the stages it describes, reaching Maturity at a point in history when the formalized study of cyclical development is still in its infancy. Some pieces of the developmental puzzle have already been contributed by Freud, Jung, Rupertini, Buhler. Piaget described how children learn, but stopped his theory at the threshold of maturity.

Montague in *Growing Young* provides another piece when he states that human beings are meant to be in an unending state of childhood development and that we are intended to remain childlike. Erikson painted a life-long picture of growth, leaving the cyclic commonalities between childhood stages and their more sophisticated grown-up versions undiscovered. Berne outlined the scripts people live and the games played to advance them, leaving some questions about how scripts develop. Daniel Levinson in *Seasons of a Man's Life* and Gail Sheehey's derivative *Passages* studied crises and patterns of adult men's lives as defined by the externals of their lives, but not why people face them, why they occur at specific ages, nor what approach might lead to successful resolution. A new science, chronobiology, is currently amassing a wealth of knowledge about the internal time-clocks found in biological organisms.

Cycles of Power's publication coincides with time when our culture is beginning to show signs of a new historical cycle, a *Third Wave*, as Alvin Toffler has christened it. Just as the first stage of each person's development is concerned with *being*, so, too, is this new stage in history concerned with issues of being. On a planetary level, we are experiencing intensely the symptoms of degeneration arising from culture cut off from the natural cyclic process. We are searching for more integral ways of being as we decide between global survival and nuclear suicide.

Additionally, the female principle is re-emerging as both women and men call for workable alternatives to one-up-one-down sex roles. Alienated from the natural world and our own natures, we seek alternates to the linear scientific model. We need a holistic science which sees humanity as a part of nature and nature as a part of humanity. We need connection with our own inner cycle because it is our connection with each other, and to all of nature and because our individual and collective survival depends upon it.

Three conscious omissions have resulted from keeping the focus of material in this edition as that of personal recovery and healthy individual development. The first is a wide range of material supporting the cyclic view of how matter is organized. Instead, interested readers will find references in the bibliography.

The second is a presentation of the cycle from conception to birth. The decision not to include it here points to its great significance. Because it is so primitive, because it has such a profound impact on later development and because it requires specialized techniques, its own separate treatment is well deserved. Informed readers will no doubt recognize themes suggesting unresolved fetal issues in the case material presented.

The third omission is an anthropological one. The cultural implications of a cyclic life process are no doubt profound. However fascinating it may prove to effectively cover how cultures currently and historically relate to this fundamental life process, to consider the implications for a culture's viability, disease patterns, incidence of violence, ability to remain cohesive, etc., it must remain a separate undertaking.

Portions of this book were researched through Group House Community in the San Francisco Bay Area, California; the members and facilitators of Mothers, Fathers and Others Who Care About Children in Minneapolis, Minnesota, now (Self Esteem: A Family Affair); Orrs Springs Healing Retreat Community, Mendocino County, California; the Eric Berne Seminars of San Francisco (formerly the San Francisco Social Psychiatry Seminars); the Schiff Rehabilitation Project (Cathexis Institute), Oakland, California; A Growing Place of Cincinnati, Ohio; and the Experiencing Enough Training, Seattle, Washington.

The completion of this manuscript was greatly assisted by the editing of Lloyd Linford, Robert Landheer, Sunny Mehler, Daniel ben Horin, Susan Ettinger Keegan, Catherine Keller, Jennie Burton, Oini la Gioia, Jean Clarke, Sally Dierks and Shiela Hartmann.

Special thanks go to my clinical sponsor, Joe Concannon, and to two special people, Gail and Harold Nordeman, who unfailingly gave of themselves under all circumstances throughout this long process.

Grateful acknowledgment is also made to the many people in this book who have generously consented to share their experiences, and who have used their own cyclic process as a potent and effective healing tool.

My thanks also to the many clinicians and educators who applied this knowledge in their work. It is through their hands that the self-published version rapidly found its way throughout the United States and to dozens of other countries. I am especially grateful to Velma Bourke, the University of Quebec, Canada, and the Indian students who translated and produced the first French language translation. It is through these people that *Cycles of Power* has taken root as a personal guidebook for grownups who felt so in name only and renamed themselves adult children.

As each individual life adjusts back to the harmony of nature's design, a much needed cultural shift begins — away from violence, substance and people abuse and addictions, the people around them also begin to organize around emotional sustenance and the satisfaction of needs. All people in every part of the world in every stage of growth deserve this environment. *Cycles of Power* is dedicated to this vision. To paraphrase Wordsworth, may we all,

> "Come forth into the light of things
> Let (our) nature be our teacher."

Pam Levin
September, 1988

The idea of return is based on the course of nature. The movement is cyclic, and the course completes itself. Therefore, it is not necessary to hasten anything artificially. Everything comes of itself at the appointed time. This is the meaning of heaven and earth.

All movements are accomplished in six stages and the seventh brings return. Thus, the winter solstice, with which the decline of the year begins, comes in the seventh month after the summer solstice . . . In this way the state of rest gives place to movement.

The I Ching

P
A
R
T

I

Nature's Design
For Life

C
H
A
P
T
E
R
1

The Cycle

The sun is almost overhead when the young woman decides it is time to lie down. Her skin is slightly pale, yet her cheeks are flushed. She looks tired as if she has carried a heavy burden on a long journey.

Her eyes are clear as she rests her head on the pillow. Her forehead grows damp and a friend at her side sponges her lightly, offering words of encouragement. She smiles in return but soon grows restless, preoccupied and fearful. Her hands become fists in a moment of intense concentration. Her breathing quickens until she is panting. She raises up and gives a cry of joy, ecstasy, relief and wonder as she beholds for the first time the child to whom she has just given birth. Gathering the still curled form to her own body, she cradles this new and helpless being, rocking it gently, her face alight with pleasure. The child's father, too, is beaming as his fingers slowly explore the tiny body. As if in thanks, the infant opens her tiny eyes, beholds her beaming parents, and utters her first affirmation of life, "NnnnnggggggYEEEAAAAA!"

At first their daughter is content to be. She cuddles close; she nurses enthusiastically; she listens and she watches, slowly becoming aware of the world around her. Shortly after her sixth month, however, being is not enough. She wants to explore her new world. She screams in frustration when unable to reach the object of her fascination. Getting it, she promptly puts it in her mouth. Day by day she becomes more competent, sitting up, crawling, climbing, seeking to know the colors, shapes and sounds around her. Keeping her world safe is a big adjustment for her parents. They are growing restless, impatient with the constant watchfulness they must maintain.

Within a few days of her second birthday, the child begins a new and puzzling pattern. She wants only what is not safe, what is out of sight or what is out of reach. She will not play with what she is given. In total fury, she lies on the floor, kicking and screaming. Her mother and father are shocked that this sweet little child, this first infant to whom they have given so much, has become so obstinate. For over a year the child continues crossing her parents, testing their reactions. Finally, slowly, her tantrums subside. She seems satisfied, as if she has accomplished something.

In the next few years, she grows tall and lean, leaving little trace of her former toddler self. She plays with other children, sharing hours creating the world as her own. She is intrigued that children are either boys or girls, and notices that grown-ups are either men or women. She sits on her father's lap with a new fascination, for he is different. He's a man and she's a girl. She pushes her mother away and seeks to divide her parents by siding with one or the other. With a mixture of relief and sadness, her parents trundle her off to her first day of school.

She is proud of the skills she is developing now. She has learned to read and write. She knows her numbers, and she knows how to argue. She will not do things the way her parents do. She takes exception to the most insignificant matters. She gets her parents to state an opinion so she can object to it. She has her own circle of friends now, most of them girls. They spend their time together playing games and arguing about rules. She has become competent, capable, skillful and opinionated. She is proficient in her girlhood world.

As time cycles on, she turns 13, and begins to develop longings and yearnings. Her breasts begin to bud. She daydreams; she wants her parents to do things for her. She wants to be close to them or to her friends, arm in arm, or leaning on one another. There is a boy who lives nearby. She cannot keep her eyes off him. The way he moves — so lithe! The shape of his chin . . . The sounds of his voice . . . She has to arrange her hair. It is as if the cycle of her life was replaying at double speed. At first she does not want to think. Next, she grows stubborn and resistant. The summer of her fifteenth year she reaches her own opinion on the subject of the male of the species. She likes him, and if her parents don't, that is most unfortunate. Slowly, gradually, as the winter comes and then the spring, she emerges as a young woman facing the world on her own, living life on her own terms.

She is lonely at first. It is like a second birth, learning to be a grown-up in a world that seems new and strange. She begins to explore, reaching out from her new home base to sense the possibilities of this promised land. She finds she needs to draw boundaries between herself and others and to develop a view of this world, which is hers. There are new skills to learn, new ways of doing things and decisions to make about being sexual. She needs time to adjust and to integrate the changes. Being grown-up is turning out to be a full-time job, and she is grateful for her friends.

The years pass quickly. The young woman spends more time at home now, with one young man and the couple's close friends who share their joys and sorrows.

The sun is nearing its highest point in the heaven when this young woman decides it is time to lie down. She is eager, tired and excited as she hears her newborn son's first sounds. Cradling him in her arms, she gains a new appreciation for her own mother. From yesterday's infant has been born the mother of today.

The Circle of Time

The wisdom in the preceding story is as old as antiquity and as modern as the new science of chronobiology. Both conclude that each of us has within us an internal developmental "clock" that provides the template or basic organizing pattern for our entire lives. Within it we can note divisions or stages, just as we note the divisions or hours on a clock. We naturally return to the beginning and repeat certain basic themes and issues because these comprise the overall design. When we remark that a grown-up is "acting like a baby" (or a two-year-old, or is going through another adolescence), our words intuitively affirm this cyclic life pattern.

However, we may not feel these returns as something natural. We may think that adults are supposed to have put away the things of childhood. We may hold a linear, rational view of life, a "factory production" mentality common in modern industrial societies. Biologists, however, have been obliged to accept that there are cyclic recurrences in the lives of animals, birds, sea creatures, plants and people. In ages past, humans shaped daily rhythms and yearly migrations according to the seasons. In modern research, set ages for the appearance of specific human life crises are revealed. These may be both physical and psychological and common to all men and women. In fact, repeating the same fundamental stages of childhood in adulthood is the healthy, normal fundamental pattern of life.

Drawing a circle, we curve the line until we return to the place where we began. Even planets move in cycles called orbits, returning to the place from which they started. Our own earth's journey takes a full year to accomplish, whereas the moon takes twenty-eight days. Water, too, has a cycle. In one phase it is home for fish in the rivers, lakes and oceans. In the next stage it collects as water vapor to form clouds and then to cleanse the air and quench the thirst of plants when it falls as rain or snow. Finally, it collects in pools, flows into creeks and rivers and runs back into the ocean to begin its cycle again.

All human bodily functions run on cyclical clocks of various lengths. One of the shortest is a complete breath. One of the longest is that from birth to death. Women's menstrual cycle is approximately twenty-eight days, the same amount of time as the moon's rotation around the earth. Like that of other animals, our metabolism runs on a daily (diurnal) cycle, including a regular rhythm of activity and rest, usually daytime activity and nighttime rest. According to biologist, Philip Holts, "The rhythmic frequency of many biological functions (heart beat, blood pressure, body temperature and hormone production) operates approximately on a twenty-four hour cycle."[1]

Scientists call these daily fluctuations circadian rhythms. In Latin, *circa* means "about" and *dies* means "time". Our mood, vigor, hand-eye coordination, as well as our ability to count, to add and to estimate time, all follow recognizable daily rhythms. The larger unfolding pattern of our lives is also rhythmic and cyclical.

This cyclic view of time, properly understood, can become a tool for living. To native Americans, the circle image is the embodiment of life they call the Medicine Wheel. To them, the wheel is not merely an accurate representation of the process of life; it is much more important. To them, it is a guide for accomplishing life goals. "For those who seek understanding," says the Indian Shaman, "the circle is their mirror." Life's purposes are accomplished by right action at the right time.

Over a decade and a half of clinical observation shows that this life cycle is composed of six stages, which return to the beginning during the seventh. Such a pattern is also validated in many ancient traditions. Egyptian and Persian holy writings, the Kabbalah and Taoist tracts all describe the seven-stage life cycle. The *I Ching,* or *Book of Changes,* a classic of Oriental wisdom states, "All things are accomplished in six stages, and the seventh brings return." Over a moment or a lifetime, the circular pattern and its stages are the same.

A full description of each stage is contained in Part II. In reading the following summary, keep in mind that more than one stage at a time can be relevant in grown-up life, a fact which is more completely discussed in Part II, Stage Seven.

The Six Basic Stages

Stage One — The Power Of Being
(Birth To Six Months)

The task of newborn babies is simply to **Be**. Their job is to seek, accept and take in nurturing and affectionate caretaking.

Symptoms. Adults going through Stage One of the cycle often experience the following signs: wanting to eat frequently, craving sweets, having mouth and light sensitivity, napping frequently, lacking concentration, thinking with difficulty, wanting to be dependent on others and wanting to be fed and touched lovingly.

Developmental Tasks. We can take advantage of this phase by carrying out the following developmental tasks:

1. Arranging for and allowing sufficient time to do nothing except rest, take in and resupply
2. Developing and expanding our emotional and physical boundaries
3. Being fed and touched
4. Taking in nourishment and affection from others
5. Being sensual
6. Creating emotional bonds with others
7. Offering nurturing and care to others

In this stage we are like a newly planted seed. Our new growth is hidden below the ground and is not apparent. We need to treat ourselves and each other tenderly so that we get what we need to grow from seed, to leaf, to flower.

Stage Two — The Power Of Doing
(Six To Eighteen Months)

The main task of older babies is to **Do.** Their job is to explore their world through their senses.

Symptoms. Adults going through Stage Two of the cycle may experience the following: wanting a variety of stimulation; wanting to see, hear, taste, touch, smell and move to explore the world; being pleasure-oriented; needing to discover our emotional roots; finding new footing; suffering tooth pain; doing new things; having a short attention span and motivational problems.

Developmental Tasks. We can take advantage of this phase by:

1. Seeing, hearing, tasting and smelling
2. Moving to explore the world without thinking about it
3. Supporting the exploration of others

In Stage Two we are like a seed just sprouting a new shoot. Our energy bursts forth anew and we can see growth almost daily. We need to stretch out and grow by sensing and doing.

Stage Three — The Power Of Thinking
(Eighteen Months To Three Years)

The main task of toddlers is to learn to think. Their job is to become separate individuals by testing and pushing against others.

Symptoms. Adults going through Stage Three may experience the following: wanting to be different from others; developing a separate position; pushing away from dependency; saying, "No!" or "I won't"; having tantrums; rebelling; feeling angry for no reason.

Developmental Tasks. We can best take advantage of this time by:

1. Pushing away from dependency
2. Testing reality, pushing against others and establishing our independence
3. Developing a separate position and learning to think
4. Providing loving limits for others going through Stage Three

At this time we are like a young plant just developing its own unique characteristics, which will become a bloom, a leaf or a branch like no other.

Stage Four — The Power Of Identity
(Three To Six Years)

The main task of preschoolers is to discover their identity. Their job is to establish who they are within a network of social relationships.

Symptoms. Adults going through Stage Four may experience: wanting to know, "Who am I?" asking many "why" questions; being preoccupied with and testing power; having interest in gender differences; experimenting with social relationships; having nightmares; developing sudden, nameless fears; feeling the urge to do something in order to find out the consequences of actions.

Developmental Tasks. We can take advantage of this phase by:

1. Learning to separate fantasy from reality
2. Testing our recognition of reality through consequences
3. Exerting our power to affect relationships by deciding who we are in a network of social relationships
4. Supporting others in establishing who they are

Plants grow in relation to their surroundings and also help create these surroundings. We also discover that as we find our place among others, we come to know ourselves.

Stage Five — The Power Of Being.Skillful
(Six To Twelve Years)

The main task of school-age children is to learn skills and work out their own set of values.

Symptoms. Adults going through Stage Five often experience the following: arguing and disagreeing with others' morals, values and methods; wanting to do it one's own way and no one else's; being preoccupied with "how to do it"; being doggedly literal and argumentative.

Developmental Tasks. We can take advantage of this phase by:

1. Learning and teaching skills
2. Arguing and disagreeing with others' ways of doing things
3. Making mistakes to find out what works

The opportunities of life unfold like flowers for those who create a way for them to do so. Doing things in our own way, we act as naturally as a flower turning toward the sun. Thus we open before us the possibilities of life.

Stage Six — The Power Of Regeneration
(Thirteen To Eighteen Years)

The main task of adolescents is to unify their personalities. Their job is to develop as sexual people.

Symptoms. Grown-ups in Stage Six often experience: having episodes of intense dependency coupled with urges to explore and be separate; being preoccupied with sexuality and with people as sexual beings; feeling discomfort or pain in sexual organs; having acne or other skin eruptions; having turbulent body changes, especially rapid fluctuations in hormones and energy levels; needing to unify into one of the various parts of our personality; and needing to develop a support system independent from others.

Developmental Tasks. We can take advantage of this phase by:

1. Briefly revisiting earlier stages
2. Experiencing more than one stage at a time
3. Integrating needs from other stages with our sexual development
4. Developing our personal philosophy
5. Pulling up roots and putting them down in the world of grown-ups
6. Supporting the passage of others through Stage Six

In this phase we are like a flower opening and developing fruit. As we accept our new level of maturity, we will begin a new cycle of growth, nurtured by what has come before. When the fruit is fully ripe, the stage is set for a new seed and a new cycle begins again.

The Power Of Recycling

This cycle of development is the fertile ground provided by nature for sowing the seeds of our life's dreams and aspirations and also for nurturing them by carrying out the developmental tasks in each stage. Returning through the stages, we build advanced skills from basic ones in the same way we build walking skills from crawling. The way to reap a bountiful harvest is to consciously carry out certain actions at critical moments.

We repeat the stages whether or not we choose to accomplish our purposes. If we choose not to use them, we will merely repeat our past with all its limiting familiarity (a condition dealt with in Chapter 2).

To nurture a successful future, we need certain emotional nutrients specific to each stage. These growth-promoting messages from others provide building blocks essential for our own healthy development and, as we exchange them with others, we build healthy relationships (see Chapter 3 and Part II).

If we choose to use the cycle to create the results we want instead of repeating the past, our first order of business is to develop a vision. How do we want our life to be? What do we want to create? Then we can use each stage to reach our goals. (For assistance with this process, turn to Part III, Chapter 1.)

The rest of this book is about how to claim, reclaim and use our fundamental birthright, our cycle of development. While reading the following chapters, notice what subject matter brings intense reactions. They are signs of material that is personally relevant. (The exercises in Part III are provided to work with them.)

<table>
<tr><td>

C
H
A
P
T
E
R
2

</td><td>

Cycle Sabotage

</td></tr>
</table>

This chapter describes two people, Bill and Dave, who are in a unique position in that they both know the vision they have for their lives and are becoming aware of a pattern in themselves that results in sabotage. After meeting them here, you can read about their foundation level developmental work in Part II.

Bill

At the age of 42, Bill married for the third time. He looked forward to the future with enthusiasm. He and his wife envisioned building a life of togetherness, in harmony with each other and with good communication leading to a profound intimacy and a happy old age. However, six months after the ceremony, Bill noticed, in desperation, he was repeating the same frustrating patterns that had already destroyed his two preceding marriages. "The first two had wound up in failure because of no communication," he said. "We had come to the point where neither one of us wanted to say what we really thought. When I think of it now, it all seems terribly sad. I'm acting with Marsha, my wife, exactly as I did with Judy and Vera before we split up. I let her decide everything. Then I pretend it's because of her I don't do anything, when actually I can see that it's my fault."

Bill has discovered that he is sabotaging his chances to realize his dream. He is running from the very intimacy he so desperately craves with his wife. And as if that isn't enough, his health is also falling apart. "Right now I'm not going to alcohol or drugs," he said, "but because I'm not getting what I want, at the same time I'm raising this asthmatic condition looking for something." By limiting our feelings and behavior, we also limit body functions even to the point of producing physical illness.

(Part II presents a complete list of physical symptoms associated with the different stages of the cycle.)

The Scenes Of Life: Rewrite Them Or Replay Them

The difficult situation in which Bill finds himself is occurring at a point in his life when he could truly attain his goal; yet it seems to him to remain frustratingly out of reach. He is discovering that we can use each stage of the cycle to manifest our vision and make our dreams come true, or we can replay the same old familiar scenes. Then, just like in a theatrical drama, our life story follows not our dreams, but our script.

According to Eric Berne, psychological scripts are similar to theatrical dramas: "The more complex operations of life can be seen as an ongoing drama that actually takes place right now, divided into scenes and acts with a buildup to a climax and ending."[2]

In later years we may have repressed and forgotten the household drama that is the basis for our script. Nonetheless, we continue to play out adaptations of it in real life. Motivated directly by childhood experiences, we may engage in a quest for characters to fit the roles demanded by the script: (1) perceiving other people in an idiosyncratic way, usually with considerable intuitive acumen and (2) tending to pick the right people to play the roles of mother, father, sibling or other significant people.[3]

Berne describes such script predicaments when he points out this fact: partners in adulthood are often drawn together by the intuitive assumption that their scripts are complementary. "There is a secret *script* contract in marriage between the two inner, younger or childlike parts of the bride and groom. Each prospective spouse is in the position of a casting director. The man is seeking a leading lady who will best play the role called for by his script, and the woman seeks a leading man to play the role adapted to hers."[4]

Inventing a plan for life is a healthy activity. As children, we imitate grown-ups, try out an assortment of roles and even conduct dress rehearsals; this imitation is a natural part of growing up. A primary task of childhood is to develop and create the foundation for future stages. Our experiences with parents and peers, and the decisions we make in response to these experiences in the first cycle of life form the base from which we respond to the pressures and possibilities of adult life. We are child-authors of the original script. We choose the players, the scenes and the acts of our life story. We create it in childhood and carry it out in adulthood.

Therefore, these childhood experiences and conclusions[5] have a profound effect long after we've forgotten them. For example, people who received pleasurable touching and affection as children may seldom consciously remember them. But in concluding that life is pleasant and good, and that other people can be trusted, they will make these childhood experiences real in every part of their adult life by continuing to be affectionate, by relating openly and spontaneously and by anticipating satisfaction. Those who lost a parent in their early years may conclude with the primitive logic of childhood, "I'm growing up and Daddy leaves me; therefore Daddy leaves me *because* I'm growing up." To avoid any more unpleasant or scary events, they may attempt to avoid growing up by sidestepping the business of their developmental stages. In leaving essential growth tasks unfinished in childhood, they fail to develop power. Their stage is set for recreating severe impoverishment and restrictions in later life.

Fortunately the life plan we make with the naive wisdom of childhood can be revised or revoked in adulthood. We can *decide* to

do nothing, to repeat earlier frustrations or to greet each stage as an opportunity to refine our performance and redirect the action. We can use past limitations, not to maintain problems, but as a starting point for creating solutions. We can:

1. Meet earlier needs and finish developmental tasks, thus ending the cycle of suffering
2. Free ourselves of cycle sabotage by changing limiting decisions and acting on our needs
3. Develop our power by carrying out the developmental tasks of our present stage

If as adults we fail to create life anew as the wheel of time turns, we content ourselves to obey childhood decisions now long forgotten. Instead of using the stages of the cycle to realize our dreams, we sabotage ourselves by recreating in the present a tragedy built on old conclusions of the past.

Culture sometimes encourages accepting limitations of personal power. In Ashley Montague's opinion, western culture has mounted a conspiracy against us. He says that human beings are not supposed to become old, that we develop best in a climate accentuating the characteristics of childhood, but that our culture tries to stifle such environments, considering them childish.[6] This point of view is also confirmed by the work of Charlotte Buhler at the University of Chicago. She points out that where society values industry and commerce to excess, the acts of people that do not serve the goals of industry and commerce, such as natural youthfulness and cyclic rhythms, are suppressed. Thus, people sacrifice their relationships with others, become out of synchronization with their own timing, become unauthentic and experience life as empty of meaning.[7]

When we give in to cultural pressures, deny our birthright and adopt behavior incompatible with the natural cycle, we become incapable of realizing our vision for life. We begin a process that is one of the most destructive to human beings. We lose our dreams, we lose our hope and become dispirited. Anne Wilson Schaef points out one such example when she says that the developmental events not completed during adolescence show up in problems of personal identity; this can lead to not knowing who we are at 40 years of age.[8]

Obedience to cultural models takes its toll on our health also. When we stifle physical needs that are part of our development at any point in the cycle, we modify biological functions, which would otherwise naturally correct themselves. We leave the way open for illness and physical deterioration. In speaking of this in regard to his asthma, Bill says, "I think it's very possible it stems from an early need. I'm really fighting opening the door to see what the problem is, but I don't see anything in my future changing unless I change. I take it for granted now that there is a problem in my character — something I have to change." (How Bill resolves this is described in Part II, Stage Two.)

How the growth process can deviate at a cellular level is no more clearly demonstrated than in cancer cells. Researchers have recently discovered a particular chemical substance, a growth-inhibiting hormone, in patients with different types of cancer such as tumors of the breast, kidneys, lungs, colon and skin. When cells are deprived of this chemical substance, they stop behaving as cancer cells and become normal. Producing these hormones seems much more likely when we transform fundamental developmental needs into growth-inhibiting mechanisms.

No matter where we are in the cycle, we can still play the scenes in any stage with boundless individuality. We can invite a standing ovation or boos and bad reviews. We can unfold a melodrama, high comedy, mystery thriller or morality play. We can: (1) develop our power or lose it and (2) realize our abilities or never take charge, wondering why life treats us this way.

Sabotage: Its Influence On The Stages

Although opportunity is always unfolding in each stage, we may experience only a sense of powerlessness, a lack of options and a feeling of diminished capacity. We may have become out of touch with our natural pattern, lost instead in one that interferes with nature's design.

"Hurry up and grow up" and "stay little" are two fundamental deviations from nature's design.[9] Living within these patterns, we misperceive or fail to see the clear and direct path that nature designed to guide us. We misinterpret our own internal impulses, thus setting the stage for problems in our relationships, our bodies and our abilities.

"Hurry Up and Grow Up" (Don't Be Dependent)

People who "hurry up and grow up" may not have had their dependency needs met or weren't offered enough protection when they were helpless babies. They decide that telling the world they need something will bring on a disaster and is therefore to be avoided until nothing worse can happen. They fail to respond to their stages in a number of ways: by acting grown-up and adequate, being rigid, requiring others to do things their way or refusing to trust others. They often keep distance from others, sometimes even acting threatening to prevent intimacy. Characteristically, they are in disagreement with others' opinions. Seldom showing or even feeling fear, they usually act angry instead.

"Stay Little" (Don't Grow Up)

People who "stay little" may not have had the support for growing up or weren't offered the structures and limits they needed to develop power in the later stages. They decided that they weren't adequate to do things for themselves and survival depended on getting others to do things for them. They fail to respond to their stages of the cycle in a number of ways: by acting little and inadequate, by trying to get others to do things they could do for themselves or by keeping others close in order to stay dependent. They often have trouble making decisions, frequently adapting instead of thinking for themselves. They seldom show or experience anger, usually acting scared instead.

Bypassing instead of finishing developmental tasks by "hurrying up" or "staying little" has the following negative consequences:

1. Some of our physical and emotional energy stays tied up and is not available for growth.
2. An underlying feeling (such as anger, fear or sadness) becomes associated with the needs and issues of that stage.
3. The personal capacities and inner character that were developing at the time are impaired.
4. Sophistication in identifying and meeting the needs of that stage do not develop because we've avoided learning experiences.
5. Development in subsequent stages is distorted.
   (Part II includes in detail some examples of this process.)

In the hope of regaining his relationship with his wife, Bill has taken the first step on the road to his liberation, one which could free him from the shackles of his past. He recalled, "Before, I didn't take my responsibilities seriously and demanded that my wife take them on. For example, I said to her, 'Okay, if you want to speak to me, I'm here.' And when I felt frustrated or unhappy in the past, I'd go out and take a drink and try to party my way out of it, but it didn't change my problem. I always said that I'd never give up and I'd hold out to the end, but now I'm willing to see where some of my problems and mistakes are. I feel I owe it to myself to work this time in order to be happy. I want to learn to be at home with myself. I'd do anything now to be comfortable inside myself. I'm finding out you don't just decide to be happy; you have to work for it."

We can all take a lesson from Bill. Like many of us, he remained a prisoner of his script — he was not free to realize his goals. But he decided to do something about it. This is the difference between winners and losers, between those who attain success and those who are content to reproduce their past. Bill has made a winning choice, one which each of us can make also.

By allying ourselves with the pattern nature evolved on our behalf, instead of opposing what has evolved since time began, we draw strength from an eternal source. By carrying out the developmental tasks associated with each stage in the cycle, we gain full use of the abilities given to each human being: to exist, to live and to **be**; to act or to do things; to be aware and to think intelligently; to know who we are and have an identity; to develop skillfulness in order to accomplish things; to regenerate or produce life anew; and to recycle or recreate power to grow.[10]

By actively developing our expertise in each of these stages, we become equal to the challenges of life at any age. We can use opportunities to carry out developmental tasks when the time comes around. We can place ourselves in a beneficial environment and make the proper adjustments to develop our own natural authority. In addition, our fulfillment becomes a resource that also benefits others.

Nevertheless, a bad start or a big mistake need not become a permanent limitation with nothing to be done about it. The cycle provides natural seasons for renewal and rebuilding. We *can* change a foundation, rebuild and reclaim our power even though life is already underway.

The Developmental Script Questionnaire[11]

Fortunately the life plan we make with the naive wisdom of childhood can be revised or revoked in adulthood because we have the power to *decide*. We can decide to do nothing, to merely repeat earlier frustrations or to greet each stage as an opportunity to refine our performance and redirect the action. We can use past limitations as the starting point for creating solutions instead of maintaining problems. We can:

1. Meet earlier needs and finish developmental tasks, thus ending our cycle of suffering
2. Open the option to act on needs and free ourselves of cycle sabotage by changing limiting decisions
3. Develop our power by carrying out the developmental tasks of our present stage

Even though we may not consciously know what choices we made in each stage of childhood, to find out, we can use the Developmental Script Questionnaire. This simple and effective method allows us to identify and define our own personal script stage by stage and thus to create a base of information that can assist us in changing the course of our life. We can uncover the foundations on which we have built our existence, the basic script we wrote for the acts and scenes of our current life. (Chapter 3 shows how to use responses to the Questionnaire to rewrite our life script.)

An Example Of The Developmental Script Questionnaire

Dave Duncan, age 50, was born and raised in the midwest. He has always lived there except for traveling in the Far East as a naval officer aboard a U.S. destroyer.

He now works for a midwestern technology company that is engaged in international trade. He travels to Europe, Japan and the Far East several times a year as part of his responsibility for multimillion dollar contracts.

"By all the usual standards, I've 'made it'," he says. "But that hasn't brought me what I'm seeking. I want to develop more personal serenity and confidence. All this outward success hasn't helped me feel okay about myself. I've always felt inferior and then worked hard to prove I'm not. I've been upwardly mobile with a tight spot in my gut. I carry a lot of tension in my back, too. I'm optimistic, I'm dedicated and I accomplish things — but I'm not nurturing enough.

"I look at my life as a struggle for feeling okay. I could feel good about myself for being inventive or for doing a good job at some things. But looking around, there are guys that just seem to feel a lot better about themselves than I feel about me. That's a real frustration," Dave asked, "How do you peel the onion, the layers of yourself, to get rid of that feeling of lacking something?"

Dave is eager to end the limitations of his script and regain his lost potential. To assess his situation more clearly, he answered the following questions. (These are repeated in Part III, Chapter 2.)

Pam Levin (PL): *Dave, when you answer these questions, fantasize and say what first comes to you without concern for accuracy, even if you feel you're making something up. This is not a test, and you will not be graded. Answer in the present, saying, 'I am' rather than 'I was.' Now, imagine you are just born. What are your parents' reactions?*

Dave Duncan (DD): *They're both very proud, very happy. My father's happy I'm a boy.*

PL: *Now, imagine you are four months old. You're hungry. You're crying and kicking. You want to be picked up, held and fed. What happens?*

DD: *My father tells my mother to do it. It's not in his head at all that he can take care of me. My mother looks at the clock to decide if it's been four hours since I was fed. If it hasn't, she walks around the block until the four hours are up, leaving me there. She can't stand to hear me cry that hard.*

PL: *So here you are an infant. All you can do is cry. What is your reaction?*

DD: *That's the hard part. I learn that if you struggle, you might not get results right away. But then you struggle even harder. And if that doesn't work, you keep trying until something works. It's a long time in between, but if you cry long enough, you'll get fed. But in any case, it's better not to feel anything.*

PL: *Now, imagine you are a toddler. You're crawling around on the floor, wanting to be picked up sometimes, getting into the cupboards and you knock over a lamp or something. What happens?*

DD: *Oh, my father would get very mad. He wasn't working much in those years; they were bad years. He'd leave the house. My mother would put me in a place where I couldn't knock anything over, maybe out on the porch by myself.*

PL: *So, your father gets mad and leaves, and your mother puts you out on the porch. What do you make of that?*

DD: *Well, if you want to do things, there's distance. I can't get support or be physically close. It's kind of a ripoff to have to do it all alone. But it doesn't count if someone helps you or you get support.*

PL: *Okay. Now, imagine you're a two-year-old. You're real interested in having your own opinion. You love to say, 'no' and 'I won't.' What happens?*

DD: *No is not allowed. It is very negative for me to say, 'No'. In fact, I have the inability to say no. I will finesse all kinds of ways, but never flat out say, 'No'. Wishy-washy is safe. No feels dangerous and scary. There'd be Pa's big verbal explosion. Nobody would hit me, though.*

PL: *Well, I'm glad about that! Now, imagine you're about four. You're interested in the difference between boys and girls, and you are figuring out which one you are. Imagine you're in the bathroom with a little girl and you want to see how she's different from you.*

DD: *Oh, I think the sky would fall. Both my parents are incredibly Victorian and very straight-laced. I would not get in the bathroom with the neighbor girl.*

PL: *Okay. Suppose you're finding out 'what happens if . . .' Suppose you take candy from a store. What happens?*

DD: *(He grinned.) There would be some kind of severe punishment. I'd get restricted to the house, maybe for a couple of days. I got up to six or seven days on occasion!*

PL: *And if you told your dad one thing and your mom another?*

DD: *They talk it out. You don't con them. They had some things mixed up but they weren't dumb. I got a lot of mixed signals, and that's tough to figure out. I think you get into a lot of insecurity because you don't know who you are or what you should be doing.* (Switching into "I" and "you" points out parts of him: a grown-up self and a younger self who needs parents.) *I really didn't do well in that developmental area, and part of what I'm trying to put into place is really, 'Who am I?' If you were born a herdsman in the seventeenth century, you knew who you were and what was expected of you. But, when you're upwardly mobile you have to be intuitive, psych that out. There was a part of my parents that was threatened if I grew. In one way, they wanted me to be powerful, and in another they were threatened if I was. There's some of that still in my head. No matter what I do, it's not enough to satisfy that feeling of being threatened.* (Here he may be saying he took his parents' threatened feelings and made them his own.) *I decided that whatever life was going to be, you had to struggle, had to figure it out and had to be tenacious as hell to do it.*

PL: *Now imagine you're between six and twelve years old. You're learning the skills of life. You're needing to learn* **how to** *. . . you want to argue and hassle to create your own values. What happens?*

DD: *Well, my father's gone a lot. He's not around to learn from. I have to learn it for myself, and everything will be a challenge. But that's okay, gets the old blood up. Focuses your attention. A lot of what I got about being a man I got from the movies. There was modeling that fear was not okay and not allowed. You work hard, you achieve and you don't be afraid. One of the poems I read when I was a Boy Scout* (Boy Scouts get into camping, etc.) *was something like this, 'Do you fear the force of the wind, the slash of the rain? Go face them and fight them, be savage again! Go hungry like the wolf, go wade like the crane! The palms of your hands will thicken, the back of your neck will tan, you'll be tired and footsore and weary, but you'll walk like a man.' I was a Boy Scout forever. I really wanted to be a man, and that was some macho stuff! The trouble is, you end up with no confidence in your value system.*

PL: *And when you're 13 to 18, becoming actively sexual?*

DD: *By then my parents left me pretty much alone. I had developed enough independence, I'd already decided to go it alone. So they* *don't really have to respond to my sexual development. One time I got in an argument with my mother about what time I should come in. She said that if I wasn't home by whatever time, she'd lock the door. I said, 'Okay. I'll just go to sleep in the hallway of an apartment building.' That was threatening enough to her, so she left the door open. In a lot of ways I didn't have much structure. So, it's hard to finish growing up. About finishing, I get about 90% done. I'm the best 90 percenter there ever was. In some ways, that's good; but then I'm still left with some feelings because I didn't finish, so I feel guilty.*

Later as a young man, Dave found a quote from Teddy Roosevelt that expressed the way he wanted to be:

> *It is not the critic who counts, not the man who points out how the strong man stumbled or where the doer of deeds could have done better. The credit belongs to the man who is actually in the arena, whose face is marred by dust and sweat and blood; who at the worst, if he fails, at least fails while daring greatly; so that his place shall never be with those cold and timid souls who know neither defeat nor victory.*

DD: *Gets a little gory with the blood in the arena, but nonetheless, I don't do well with small projects. I get bored if I'm under-challenged and I don't do well. If I can get my teeth into something that I feel is worth doing, then I'm much more likely to succeed.*

Although Dave's answers are not necessarily a perfect historical recollection, they nonetheless reflect his understanding of the key parts of his life plan and how it relates to the natural cycle of development. Much of the legacy he carried from childhood was positive. He points out, "It's easy for me to be the optimist, to see the good parts. I know how to work hard, I have a good education, I'm a good employee, I'm dedicated and I know how to accomplish things. Those are all good and admired qualities in this culture. And I'm good at figuring things out. I can psych things out, and that's the reason I'm good at this cross-cultural work I'm doing now, in Europe, Japan and China."

The most pressing problem with his script was being stoic and missing intimacy. "You don't show your feelings and you're secretive," he said. "But it's better to share and talk. And to know what you feel. When I was young I had the biggest 'don't feel' message around.

"I'm tired of carrying this feeling that I lacked something when I was growing up, and I want to come to terms with the not okay part of me in a constructive way."

Having outlined the key parts of his personal developmental design, Dave decided to use the natural return to Stage One to change the pattern that interfered with nature's plan to reclaim his *Power to Be.* (See Part II, Stage One for a description of this process.)

When Dave is finished in Stage One, his answers to this questionnaire can guide his work in other stages. (For readers who want to find out about their own developmental scenes, this questionnaire can be found in Part III, Chapter 2.)

Chapter 3 discusses how to begin letting go of an uncomfortable but nonetheless familiar past and going into the new and unfamiliar territory where our dreams become possible. The challenge is to rechannel our energies from opposing, avoiding or sabotaging the cycle to openness and cooperation with the revolutions of our development, trusting that nature's design has our best interest at heart. The rest of this book is about that great adventure.

CHAPTER 3

Seeds Of Power

Deviating from nature's plan is self-sabotage because we fail to use the natural opportunities for developing the power and abilities we need to succeed. Without even knowing it, we recreate in the present an ongoing drama that is based on unhappy past conclusions.

Beginning to change that circumstance may seem a difficult step when we truly believe we can't, or we shouldn't, or that the danger will be overwhelming. Even though each of us is capable of solving problems and reaching our goals, we may be stuck in responding to internal messages saying quite the opposite.

Such an internal voice, full of parental advice and admonitions about *money* (a clue to Stage One) has been plaguing Dave Duncan. This voice also tells him he should be *doing* — "getting straight, that

I should have things all worked out." Listening to that, he *feels* inadequate and incapable even though he knows better.

Mitch Salzman's internal voice only reinforced his burnout as a speech and language therapist. He felt drained, saying, "My school principal wasn't on me, but I was keeping myself under some kind of observation in my mind. I never allowed myself to take compliments with a feeling that it's okay to receive."

Beatrice Bach is a person committed to her family and her church, yet she lived under advice that sounded like family voices telling her to be perfect, do right, impress the neighbors, appear to look good and never to show faults. She said, "I should love and honor my parents, and yet I didn't always. The voices said, 'That's terrible, and you a Christian girl; you'd better do something about that'." So intense were the voices at one point that, in an effort to turn them off, Bea attempted suicide. She revealed, "I wanted to kill that part of me and finally be done with it. But I really didn't want to die." Bea's desperate attempt testifies to the incredible power of negative programming. Invalidating ourselves internally is a way we stay locked into script limitations, keeping ourselves powerless and inadequate instead of active and effective.

Affirmations

Affirming messages[12] are powerful, positive phrases we can use to replace negative ones. By deliberately repeating new messages to counter those renouncing our capabilities, we begin to claim the power that is our birthright. We begin to take charge of our minds.

Affirmations are messages that reinforce adequacy, give permission and support our natural developmental process. Some examples are, "My anger is okay," "It's okay for me to change," "It's all right for me to get what I need," "I'm an important person and other people are important, too," "I am lovable," and "It's okay for me to feel what I feel."

Affirming messages are so potent that they can even produce changes in the cardiac and respiratory rate of patients in a coma. Repeating positive phrases to ourselves can produce similar results even at the deep and primal levels of our lives. (To aid in discovering your own personal affirmation, turn to Part III, Chapter 3 for an exercise entitled "Using the Think Structure to Create Your Personal Affirmations".)

Using affirmations is a beginning step in changing our script. We still need to change basic decisions and complete developmental tasks within the stages, making the new message the foundation for our developmental design instead of just something we say. To achieve this new consciousness in adulthood we need to build on childhood experiences rather than overcome them. For example, grown-up knowledge of the world is built on toddler experiences when we first explore the world on our hands and knees. Later, we add walking skills and then we can run. All these contribute to our grown-up navigational abilities. Completing developmental tasks is how we can translate an affirming thought into basic bodily knowledge.

The right surroundings to do this are just as important for adults as they are for children. In the proper environment we can thrive, making real our potential for development that we might not otherwise accomplish. To flower as an individual, for example, we need an environment made safe by effective limits and plenty of affection. (Part II contains a stage-by-stage description of these surroundings.)

Changing basic parts of a life plan also requires time and energy. For example, if the first version of a script did not include creativity and now you want to become a painter, you won't become Picasso or Grandma Moses by tomorrow morning. Capacities must be developed, skills honed and muscles trained. Or, you may want to update your methods of handling anger, wanting to be effectively angry when you need to, instead of feeling guilty. You'll need time to learn skills that other people have developed over years of experience. Grant yourself the time and support you need to learn. You needn't dawdle; but don't be surprised when it takes time to catch up.

A life plan is rewritten, not with one swift stroke, but by stages, piece by piece. Knowing that the recycling process will bring up issues and make them readily available for reworking without a lot of digging, and knowing each stage is normal, you can be encouraged. You can open up and relax. The idea is not to get through the stages faster but to develop your present potential by doing current tasks.

Dealing effectively with the present stage is the best way to prepare for the ones to follow. The important thing is not to wait for the ideal set of circumstances, but simply to *start.*

Before you go on to Part II, remember that all the stages in the cycle are relevant to your life even though only one of them may seem so now. Read through all of them even though you'll refer to specific stages for your life now. Then go on to Part III for specific exercises for developing all powers of the cycle. Some general pointers to remember as you travel through any stage of the cycle follow below.

Pointers To Aid Your Success

You Can Do It. You can solve problems. It really is possible.

You Do Know. You know what you need at some level. The only people who don't know are those who are brain damaged or drugged. It's okay for you to know.

Decide To Think. Decide to think about it. This step is so basic and obvious it is often overlooked. You are not just what you are feeling; you can think also.

Do Something About It! When you're uncomfortable, do something about it. It's not necessary to go around hurting.

The Discomfort Of Becoming Aware. When you begin to identify a problem you may feel as if you're getting more uncomfortable when you are merely becoming more aware of discomfort that was already present. What appears to be greater distress is really greater awareness.

When It Doesn't Work. Problem solving is a process of trial and error. When you decide to do something, just do it. It doesn't have to be the best thing or even the right thing. You can learn a lot from things that don't work right away. Take the opportunity to appreciate the richness of the results, whatever they are. This is important because if you have the right to fall down sometimes, you have the room to change.

Response-ability: Own It! Take responsibility for the problem. If you try to use the external situation as an excuse for your behavior, you may drive away the support you need. You won't be in a position to get what you need because your lack of responsibility blocks the pathway. This will be easy to do if you remember it's okay to blow it!

Be A Skeptic! You don't have to be a firm believer that you're going to lick this thing, "by jiminey"! Be as skeptical as you wish. However, a problem-solving position is essential. You can be like a scientist conducting an experiment: skeptical, but careful, conscious and open to a solution.

When Rigor Mortis Sets In. Total nonproblem solving behavior looks like either total psychosis or rigor mortis. The point is, you're always doing something about what you need, so find that kernel of doing and start there.

Don't Cheat Yourself. There's *trying* to solve a problem and then there's solving it. You know the difference, so there's no sense trying to fool anybody. You'll only fool yourself. The point is to stop cheating yourself.

Starting In Is Invigorating! Take the initiative about your problems. Don't wait for someone else to notice and do something about it. So much more time is wasted not getting what you need and being needlessly uncomfortable.

Give Up Playing Games. The level of knowing what you need is not the game level. You need to stop playing games in order to know.

"Plumb Tuckered." You have to have energy to do it. So, if you're too busy or too tired, curl up in bed with your nice flannel blanket and your thumb. You'll feel better in the morning. No problem solving process works by magic when you're "plumb tuckered".

The Jackpot! You may experience your resistance greatly increasing as the problem comes more into focus. If this happens, it's a sure bet you're on the right track. You hit the jackpot!

It's Your Show. Set up your new situation the way you want it to be. That doesn't mean don't listen to anybody else's advice; it's just another way of saying it's your show.

Feeling You're The Problem. You may feel that you yourself are the problem, rather than that you're a person who has a problem.

During stress our problems are often brought out, activated and energized. However, you can still think about what's going on. You are much more than just your problems.

Before starting the second part of this book, decide which stages in the cycle are of utmost concern to your life now. Read the ones that interest you first and the rest afterwards. Study them all. That way you can follow your own recycling process all the better.

When you've rewritten your personal life plan to be in harmony with your natural cycle of development, you will have:

1. "Un-stuck" physical and emotional energy that was tied up, making it available currently
2. Resolved anger, fear or sadness that were associated with your needs in that stage
3. Repaired any injury to the abilities you were developing at the time
4. Developed sophistication and expertise in identifying and meeting the needs of that stage
5. Ended the limiting effect of that pattern on the stages that follow it

Congratulate yourself. You deserve it.

PART II

The Seven Stages
Of The Cycle

The Developmental Cycle

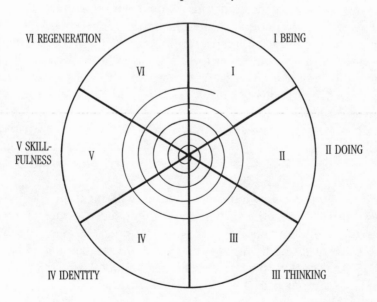

VI REGENERATION

I BEING

VI

I

V SKILL-
FULNESS

V

II

II DOING

IV

III

IV IDENTITY

III THINKING

Introduction

In this second section, each chapter begins with a list of the ages and life circumstances that are of particular significance for each stage. They are followed by six key affirming messages, a summary of normal symptoms and the signs of deviation for that phase. The ages listed in the introduction denote common major and minor recycling ages that are typical of that stage.

The next part of each chapter describes how we set our stage and common script decisions that limit grown-up development.

The following part describes cycle sabotage in detail. The games people are likely to play and the physical symptoms we may develop when we sabotage the cycle by avoiding the tasks are listed.

The last section in each chapter is about how to reclaim power. Here various people tell about their own experiences in stopping cycle sabotage. They describe their script (hurry up and grow up, stay little) and how they created the conditions that permitted them to free their energy and come back to nature's plan.

Many of them completed foundation level work they had left unfinished from childhood through a therapeutic process called corrective parenting. Their descriptions are included here for information only. Foundation level work is only to be undertaken with competent help, with safe limits and plenty of affection, and in a protected environment. (Turn to Part III for methods and exercises readers can use.)

Remember, the needs of each stage are best met within the natural rhythm of the cycle. Each season of the cycle is part of nature's gift. Using nature's plan as an ally, everything — including the most cherished dream — becomes possible.

Note: In the following sections you will meet people who generously consented to share their experiences. Some of their names have been changed at their request. As you become conversant with the themes of each stage, notice that themes from other stages peek through. These are clues about what work people need to do in other stages.

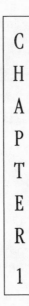

| C |
| H |
| A |
| P |
| T |
| E |
| R |
| 1 |

Stage One:
The Power Of Being

All things in the world come from being.
Lao Tzu (Sixth Century BC)

Summary

This stage has particular significance for those who are:
- just born to six months old
- age 13, 26, 39, 52, 65, 78, 91
- age 19, 38, 57, 76, 95
- tired, hurt, vulnerable or ill
- in periods of rapid change or growth

- suffering a personal loss
- taking care of an infant
- pregnant
- in any time of stress
- just beginning any process

Affirmations

It's okay for you to be here, to be fed, touched and taken care of.

You have a right to be here!
I'm glad you're a (girl-boy).
I like to hold you, to be near you and to touch you.
You don't have to hurry, you can take your time.
Your needs are okay with me.

Normal Symptoms

Symptoms can include wanting to eat frequently, having difficulty thinking, craving sweets, having mouth sensitivity, napping frequently, lacking concentration, wanting to be dependent on others, especially to be lovingly fed and touched.

Deviations

Hurry Up. This means feeling little like an infant, being scared and needy but acting grown-up and angry instead.

Stay Little. This means feeling like an angry grown-up but acting like a scared baby while waiting for somebody to guess we need something.

Developing The Power Of Being

Whenever we repeat Stage One, developing *The Power of Being,* our urges to think or to act are greatly diminished and sensations are intensified. We become alive to pain or itching in our mouth, throughout our entire gastrointestinal system, and all over our skin. We may become preoccupied with sensual gratification or absent minded and unable to concentrate. We may try to satisfy these gnawing sensations by chewing a pencil or gum, or wanting to smoke. We may rub or scratch our skin to provide stimulation.

We experience the need for more sleep, we want frequent naps, we go to bed early and get up late. We seek recognition for the way we *are* rather than for our deeds and accomplishments. Words alone don't satisfy our needs. We may need to snuggle up close to a loved one to feel that needed security.

Marge

Just after reaching her longtime goal of being promoted to senior vice-president of a major accounting firm, Marge Bennington exclaimed, "For about the last month I can't seem to keep my hand from going to my mouth. I want nothing more than to be close all the time.

"Yesterday I had a full list of things to do, but instead I spent hours cuddling up with my eight-year-old daughter. We played with a little toy music box she's had since she was a baby. I'm even eating meals lying on the sofa with my family all around. Besides, that way I can see what's on other people's plates. When they feed me tidbits of food, it seems to taste better. Also, I'm eating more often. I don't like big meals so much; I'd rather eat a little and eat all of the time. If somebody else fixes it for me, I feel so good I almost glow.

"When I went to the grocery store the other day, I had a hard time deciding what to buy. Usually I'm a good organizer, but lately I'm likely to stand there looking at all that food and wanting somebody else to tell me what to do, or, better yet, do it for me. And you know how I like parties! But now my idea of a good time is to stay home all weekend, curl up in bed with a novel and get a massage. I know better than to resist needing to take a break. If I fight the need to regroup, the next likely thing is I'll lose my checkbook, my wallet or my keys. Then I'll get sick."

Harold

Harold Simmons, a grandfather of twelve children, described similar symptoms as he moved from his large house to a small apartment. "My latest grandchild was just born," he said, "and he's a beauty. The two of us are in the same boat. We've got no hair and no teeth and we're too helpless to take care of ourselves. We gotta figure out who all these new folks are and whether or not we can trust them. I can hold him for hours. It's my greatest pleasure and it makes life worth living. I wouldn't miss this for the world."

In Stage One, life is back to the first priorities, simply being *alive,* sustaining life, keeping body and soul together, handling feelings and learning how to enjoy living. Issues of helplessness, trust, mistrust, adequacy, satisfaction and sensuality become preoccupations. Basic needs for food, money, love and sex are dominant concerns. Our dreams hold images, which are misty and blurred, containing vague often unrecognizable shapes of light or shadows.

Before attempting to do anything, our inner strength needs development. Making solid bonds and sustaining connections to supportive people in the present is how we lay the foundation for future mastery. Otherwise, we can't afford to expand beyond our current, increasingly restrictive circle. To avoid this is to limit our potential for being.

The ages listed for Stage One are only guidelines. Listen to your body and let it tell you when you are in Stage One. Remember, being in Stage One will work for you as long as you carry out the tasks associated with it.

Regardless of how old we are, each time we experience the symptoms of Stage One, we need to accomplish the following Developmental Tasks that strengthen our being:

1. Recognize the existence of ourselves and others apart from our acts or accomplishments
2. Be taken care of, treated with consideration and resupplied
3. Create emotional bonds with others based on trust
4. Touch and be touched
5. **Be** without forcing to **do**
6. Be nourished and nurtured, and do the same for others
7. Be sensual

(Exercises for dealing with these needs are listed in Part III, Chapter 4.)

Setting The Stage For The Power Of Being

We first experience Stage One, or oral needs, during the first six months of life. As babies, we need both physical and verbal stimulation: to be fed, touched, talked to and held with affection. Through this contact, we receive the nutrients necessary to build our body cells and set our systems in motion. At the same time our innermost boundary, our gut, and our outermost boundary, our skin, are stimulated. These body sensations constitute our first awareness of having a *physical* existence. Based on this first knowledge, we make decisions about who we are, what life is like and what it will take to survive.

As babies we are helpless. We have only our cry to let the world know we need something. If we could talk, we might say, "I exist! I can feel! I need and want! I am! Feed me, touch me, love me, play with me!" As babies we like to hear positive messages, such as "You're growing so well", rather than the negative "You're getting too heavy to hold". We prefer, "You're doing such a good job learning how to eat" to "You're making such an awful mess" or "You're such a burden". At this young age, the response of others to our crying signal tells us whether we are really encouraged to be here, to exist and to be real.

Getting fed and touched *is* survival for infants because it stimulates the body's sustaining systems. Digestion, respiration, elimination, immunologic and circulatory systems all must function well if life is to continue. When we are lovingly touched, our skin says, "Mmmmmm, nice" and a series of chemical changes tell our other organs to "keep on going". We then breathe more deeply, send more oxygen through our blood, manufacture white blood cells to clean up debris, fight off infection and eliminate waste.

Our infant nervous system protects us through a series of life-supporting reflexes, such as (1) crying: "Help! I need something!" (2) gagging: "Oops, wrong tube. I don't want to breathe in that milky stuff!" (3) dancing reflex: "I'll curl into a well-protected fetal position." (4) sucking: "Mmmmmm, move that warm, life-giving milk into my tummy." (5) rooting: "Where is that nipple? I know it's around here someplace!" and (6) feeling alarm: "What was that noise? It woke me out of a sound sleep!"

Gender is a decisive factor in our status and the kind of treatment we receive as infants. As newborns, the announcement of our birth answers the primary question: "Is it a boy or a girl?" We are then stroked and fed in gender-related patterns. Boy babies are often handled vigorously and stimulated more than girls. This kind of early handling supports the boy later viewing himself as sturdy and active. Girls may, on the other hand, come to see themselves as passive and fragile.

"He's a tough little guy" is communicated by not giving boys what they need when they cry. "She's such a tiny, delicate little thing" is communicated to girls by anticipating their needs even before they cry. Thus, sex roles are part of cultural patterning right from the cradle. Infant boys are in training to acquire the traits of the master class (aggressiveness) whereas infant girls are trained in the traits of subjugation (passivity).

These early experiences and the decisions we make in response to them are the foundations on which we base all later personality development. Conclusions, such as, "I have to fight for every ounce", "It's not okay for me to be here", "It's dangerous to let the world know I need anything", "There's not enough" and "Pleasure is dangerous and to be avoided", are all stored in our sustaining systems where they direct the activities of our bodies in later life. For example, if as infants we missed the physical closeness that satisfies the skin's hunger, and did not learn to be comfortable with rhythmic, voluntary and involuntary movements, as adults we will experience related grown-up problems with the quality of our life and with sexuality.

From this first stage on, we will periodically need to recharge our *Power of Being* with loving, safe, playful and sensual contact and emotional bonding with others. As we grow older, we add other, more sophisticated forms of physical contact, such as a hug, a hand shake or even a massage. We even learn rules about when, how and with whom contact is acceptable.

Whether at three months, or thirty-nine years, nothing recharges our *Power to Be* as quickly and completely as physical affection and emotional bonding, especially being held and touched with love.

Cycle Sabotage In Stage One

Sometimes we respond to Stage One by attempting to avoid feeling anything — even feeling alive. Afraid to let the world know we need something, we may "hurry up and grow up" and cover fear with anger to protect ourselves. Instead of seeking emotional and physical closeness, we become rigid and depressed, using a black cloud of bad feelings to keep distant from others. Or we may respond by becoming busier and more intellectual, attempting to avoid the world of feelings and sensations altogether and allowing only thoughts and concepts to intrude on our consciousness.

We may also avoid Stage One by "staying little", covering angry feelings with fear. Instead of telling others what we need, we become increasingly passive, doing nothing except aggravating our discomfort and agitation while waiting for others to discover what is wrong.[13]

Stage One Games[14]

When we deny our need to be nurtured, we are motivated to play games in relationships, to justify problems instead of asking for what we need. We may whine or suffer around anyone who represents a possible source of nurturing. We become preoccupied with grown-up worries, insisting that the reason for the problem is lack of enough . . . (time, food, money, love, sex, etc.). The following games[15] are typical of, but not limited to, this first stage in the Cycle of Development:

1. **Indispensable** is a competency game we play when our infant experiences have encouraged us to decide that we have no right to be. We earn our right to exist by being perfect or better than anybody else just to stay equal. We get everybody dependent on us but keep our own needs for others a secret.

2. **Addict** is played when infant experiences leave us feeling on the brink of death. We have decided that others are never dependable and that we are helpless and unable to take care of ourselves. Instead of asking straight, we extort caring from others by putting ourselves on the brink of destruction.

3. **Obesity** is played if, as infants, we weren't allowed to eat as much or as little as we needed because we were either deprived of food or force fed. We eat in response to anger, not hunger.

4. **Bag O'Bones or Anorexia** is the corollary to obesity. The dynamics are the same except we starve rather than fill up in response to anger.

5. **Kick Me** is played if, as infants, we had to be in pain in order to get our needs met. We invite pain instead of comfort when we need something.

6. **Chain Smoker** is often played if, as infants we were kept in a perpetual state of anxiety about supply. Our motto in this game might be, "If it isn't in my mouth right now, I'm not going to get it." We smoke, when what we really need is affection, food, comfort, connection or rest.

7. **Indigent** is played when we think we must stay needy to keep contact. Often as infants we were held and fed only until we were full. Then we lost contact when we were returned to our rooms, cribs, playpens or plastic carriers.

The Body Language Of Being

Whenever we leave undone the developmental tasks which develop our *Power to Be*, we exhibit disturbances in our sustaining systems and nervous systems. The following physical problems are typical of avoiding Stage One tasks:

1. **Generalized Body Tension Or Generalized Anxiety.** This is the most common and also the earliest symptom of our needs building from Stage One. There is no specific place that feels tight and no particular stimulus for the anxiety; we just feel tense all over and anxious about nothing apparent.

2. **Skin Problems**. When we need touching, rest or need to eliminate toxins but don't do it, our skin lets us know. We may develop cases of psoriasis, blemishes or boils, or an outbreak of cold sores or herpes. (Or as one woman put it, "My skin is screaming.") These are all ways in which the skin says, "Touch me," "Feed me better," "Don't feed me so much," or "Let me rest."

3. **Eating Imbalances.** We may eat because we misinterpret a gnawing, empty sensation as hunger for food instead of a hunger to be touched. Some of us crave sweets. Others may turn off hunger sensations entirely and eat too little. Still others may smoke to avoid feeling hungry.

4. **Disturbances In Our Sustaining Systems.** We don't sustain life without our digestive, circulatory, respiratory, eliminative and immunologic systems. Clinical evidence shows that unmet Stage One survival needs ultimately show up as sustaining system symptoms, such as a hyperactive bowel or constipation, chronic nausea, inability to process food, frequent infections, nagging cough, bronchitis or asthma.

5. **Breast Symptoms.** Breasts, our source of nourishment as infants, can be a source of trouble when we deny our need to be nurtured. Breast lumps, cysts or tumors are sometimes connected to Stage One needs. Common reactions are: being fascinated with or having fear of women's breasts, controlling "breast energy" by keeping the rib cage frozen and not showing affection. (One 19-year-old woman, estranged from her family began lactating. "I think I'm trying to feed myself," she said.)

You may have some untapped power potential to develop in Stage One: (1) if "Not enough," "Can't be effective," "Afraid I'll be inadequate," or "Afraid I'll lose what I have," (with no apparent reason) are recurrent themes for you, or (2) if you act as if someone insisted, "Don't be," "Don't feel," or "Don't have needs."

Reclaiming The Power Of Being

In the following section, men and women who experienced cycle sabotage in Stage One describe how they were failing instead of using this phase to realize their goals and satisfy their dreams. They tell how they grew beyond self-imposed limits from their Stage One script decisions. The first element uses the affirmations designed to provide the social nutrients necessary for healthy development in Stage One. The second aspect is taking in the nurturing necessary to complete basic tasks left unfinished from childhood. The third key to their success involves working directly with the vital functions or sustaining systems of the body through affectionate physical contact and food — the most direct way to meet Stage One needs and create sufficient security to allow ourselves to **Be**.

Valerie

A bright, energetic nursery school teacher, Valerie Schraft (VS), had goals and vision that involved a fulfilling relationship with a man, and money — two areas in which she experienced chronic limitation. Currently she was involved with a married man who was, of course, not available to be the life partner she wanted. Tired of not having any money, she longed for a career change, but felt she lacked the ability and financial backing to implement it. The last year had even brought physical symptoms similar to ones she'd had before; once in adolescence and again at age 26. She had been depressed, and had digestive problems, eczema and erratic eating patterns. Valerie decided it was time to resolve this, whatever it was. Her description follows.

VS: *Although I'm not overweight, I eat a lot. I feel a big need to take it all in. Also, it's been almost inconceivable to me that people just trust naturally. I watch people and I see that it's true. I used to say, 'Well, at least I don't have a trust issue.' But the bottom line is always what keeps you from doing what you need to do, and the bottom line is always trust, being really close to somebody. I wouldn't cry in front of anybody for a long, long time.* (I assume she means because she didn't trust others' responses.)

I took care of other people. They'd confide in me but I wouldn't confide in them. I was afraid to let them see that I was less than perfect. Now I'm realizing the issue is one about not trusting.
PL: *What have you done about that so far?*
VS: *All my life I've worked on the theory that I'm too much for any one person* (part of her infant decision about **Being**). *So I've decided which parts of myself I'll let out of the box I've kept myself in* (the restrictions on **Being** she experiences).

To change that I've done several things. One is that I've been working it out slowly, taking my time instead of hurrying. Another is letting you hold me. And I've been finding out I don't have to be any

certain way by being miserable and crying a lot. Finding out that was okay, I'd let another part out of the box and see what happened.
PL: *What kinds of support helped you go ahead and do it?*
VS: *Having invitations to be held and to relax has been real important. I needed encouragement. And talking about bonding, that it's okay for us to have a close, emotional bond, was a major step.*

Now being taken care of is something I look forward to and enjoy. My voice goes soft when I think if it; although, I think there's still some scare for me. (By saying 'some scare,' she is still creating distance from her fear.) *Still, I can almost relax enough to fall asleep. There's a real sense of letting go. I hold a lot of tension in my body and my back, and when you hold me and massage those places, I really feel nurtured.*

When Valerie first began to reclaim her potential for **Being**, she faced a big issue about what price she'd have to pay if she let someone take care of her. She said, "Slowly I began realizing that holding me has its own reward for you. That's something I understood when I held one of the kids at school. But when I was the one being held, I thought I'd have to entertain you, or think a lot or give up being competent and make some sacrifice to be vulnerable."

Valerie believes she was taken care of custodially as an infant. "I was fed, changed, all that, but I didn't experience that spontaneous playing, loving and being nurtured. My mother was competing with me for my father's attention during my infancy. I was the girl after two boys and my father really wanted a girl. At the same time he was having an affair with someone else and wasn't giving my mother any attention. He'd lavish attention on me and my mother got jealous."

Valerie also needed to learn about bonding with others. Slowly, by repeatedly being held and allowing herself to relax, she experienced and acknowledged what a bond is, "To allow my body to melt into you and not have boundaries, to cuddle up, feel comfortable and relax. That was a big barrier for me to cross because I had closeness and nurturing all mixed up with sex. I needed to learn that I could be taken care of without taking on a lot of other people's sexual tensions. I needed to learn that I can even cuddle close to your breast and not have it be scary."

Valerie also needed to learn one of the healthy developmental tasks of infants: to take in nourishment. "Taking a bottle of milk was the hardest part of what I needed to learn," she said, "and it turned out to be the most significant lesson, because in letting you feed me I learned that you would take care of me."[16]

Reclaiming the power potential she had left in infancy, Valerie has expanded her life. She explained, "I'm not always protecting myself, being defensive and acting like I don't need anything. I'm more open in asking for what I need. I can ask friends to come over, to go somewhere with me, to come and cuddle, to spend the day together or to help me out with a project. I was always there for other people, and that gave me a certain power over them. Now, that tension is gone because we have reciprocity, give and take.

"My mental state is often reflected by the kind of shape my house is in. When it's totally in chaos, clothes all over the place or a sink full of dishes, then I know something is going on. I'm not just being busy. I'm more likely being *hungry.* Now, when that happens I'm allowing myself time to *not* do things. I'll sit on the couch and stare into space. When I feel overwhelmed, I call a friend or take myself out to dinner. I allow myself to feel vulnerable. I can say, 'Will you come over and spend the day with me?' or 'How about a back rub or a massage?'

"A close relationship, having someone know who I really am and not just the image I put out, brings a lot of opportunities I didn't see before. There was part of me, before these changes, that didn't believe I could be a major consultant. I never would have allowed myself vision before. Now I am considering it as a possibility. Before my life was under control, but only in a very limited sphere. Now that I have more trust, I can expand my boundaries."

Dave

Dave Duncan (see Chapter 2 for his answers to the Developmental Script Questionnaire) has some physical symptoms that are clues to Stage One. He carries tension in his upper back and has a tight belly. He believes these are symptoms of fear.

"When I was younger," he says, "fear was an emotion that was not allowed. I'd like to be able to let go of my inner anger and be more nurturing. I have learned as a youngster to be stoic and to keep my feelings hidden. I know it's better to share and talk, but I can't share if I can't feel. I want to trust people, but I don't know how. I want to feel, to trust, to share."

As part of recovering and developing his *Power to Be,* Dave arranged to be held and taken care of many times. "At first I kept thinking I should be doing something," he said. "I was so reassured to hear, 'You're not supposed to do anything except to take in what you need, to get taken care of, to decide to be alive and to feel everything you feel'."

Soon he began relaxing and feeling everything more intensely. In addition, he felt good about himself. "I feel better able to choose what I'll do and what I won't," he said. "Also, being taken care of has helped me understand the difference between nurturing and sexual contact. Even knowing there's a difference has been important. When I grew up, boys didn't learn how to treat a woman or how to deal with their sexuality or their bodies. Being able to be alive and to feel is the first step in that process."

People whose experiences in infancy formed the basis for "hurry up and grow up" show patterns similar to Valerie's and Dave's. Their infant self is *scared,* especially of helplessness, immobility or annihilation. They protect their scared self with angry behavior or depression, both ways to keep people distant. Their decision is, "Don't tell the world I have needs until nothing worse can happen."

They act powerful, strong, scared, hard, cold, old, independent or persecuting in order to protect their scared, needy, helpless, hungry and dependent infant. Confronting their covering behavior only deepens their need to protect themselves. They avoid intimacy unless they are in a situation where they can work through an infant fear of helplessness.

One man described his feeling, "I've never been as scared as I was when I faced my own infant fear — not even when I was a bomber pilot in World War II."

If you decided to "hurry up and grow up" as an infant, you *may* need to develop a new trust relationship. If so, you can take your time, be taken care of and gain the experiences you need to build a new foundation for expanding your *Power to Be.*

Mitch

Mitch Salzman, a 34-year-old active, athletic speech and language therapist, was working with children when his stress level reached emergency proportions. First he flunked a course at graduate school, next his mother died and then he received a new school assignment; all these occurred within a short span of time. He felt he'd been doing his best and it wasn't good enough. He was burned-out. Even his relationships with women were wrong. Somehow they always wound up platonic, instead of sexual. Mitch wondered, "Am I missing the link one needs to have a successful sexual relationship?"

At first he thought it was his looks (he was born with a bilateral complete cleft palate, which has been surgically repaired). He felt vulnerable, with no backup or support. His thinking became judgmental. He was having trouble **Being**.

When most of his friends married, he said, "Yes, I want what they have! Let me at one of those!" He decided to search for that missing link. "What was scary was the feeling of rejection I had to face, not Mommy and Daddy rejection, but specifically rejection by members of the female gender. When I thought about creating that emotional bond with a woman, immediately I'd think about my looks. Something about my emotional hunger was giving me a feeling of inadequacy."

Besides these clues, Mitch's body was sending him messages, too. He was 26 years old when he found out he had an ulcer, although he'd had stomach problems for a while. More recently he'd developed a scalp infection and lost his hair. "I was trying to achieve lofty goals to compensate for feeling inadequate about my palate condition," he said. "I was criticizing myself internally. If I did something right, I'd always find something wrong to negate it. I'm not a physical fitness buff, but when I felt this way, I had to run or jog or swim or play tennis, anything. I couldn't sit still; I'd be crawling out of my skin, like overdosing on sugar or coffee. That energy was my unfulfilled needs, not here and now, but way back down the corner and around the block about twenty years or more."

Mitch decided to regain his undeveloped *Power of Being*. He began by working on his anger, which he soon discovered was motivated by hunger for touch, affection and nourishment. He began to express anger in a group where he had good support and protection from other people. He began by pounding on pillows.

Then he seemed to grow younger and younger, curling into a fetal position and sounding much like a hungry baby. Everyone picked him up and helped hold him while he sucked on a bottle of milk, the first one of his life! (As an infant Mitch had been fed with a dropper — he was unable to suck without inhaling the milk.)

He described this experience as a gut/mind fusion. "I experienced a personal renaissance," he said, "as if I'd been reborn. I created some kind of physical connection making me feel less vulnerable and defensive, so that I could go back and do what I didn't do in infancy. When I was a baby, I was in the hospital alone. I remember crying and crying, knowing I was alive, but not wanting to be there. I was so lonely, I wanted to be held."

Because Mitch hadn't been able to suck as a baby does, he needed to learn to *take in,* as infants do. That new foundation was what he needed to expand his *Power of Being* and build his sexuality as an adult.

"After I got what I wanted, was held and fed," he said, "I realized that's what the anger had been about. Now I've filled up the hole where the anger was, the anger that was driving people away."

Mitch's infections and hair loss have subsided and so has his constant self-criticism. "I've also changed what I value," he said. "I'm not so interested in how a woman looks, but in the kind of relationship we can have together."

At a party recently, Mitch was delighted that people wanted to be close to him, to laugh and joke with him. "They heaped all kinds of praise on me, and I was able to lap it up, to feel it in my body! I love feeling people liking me."

People whose infant experiences formed the basis for "stay little" may show a pattern similar to Mitch's. They balk at directly expressing their needs. Instead, they try to get others to do something for them without having to ask, a pattern usually begun in infancy where they received reinforcement for being passive[17] or for not initiating when they needed something.

Mitch decided not to initiate because of his cleft palate. Others may not initiate because they were overfed. "My parents kept insisting I eat whether I was hungry or not," one woman said. "As a grown-up I often felt angry when somebody asked me over for dinner. I actually had to remind myself they weren't force-feeding me!"

"Stay little" is based on an infant feeling of *anger*, often from being interfered with or smothered, instead of mothered or fathered. Babies protect their angry infant self with fear, and may act incompetent to keep others close.

Some people had different infant experiences with men than with women so that they use both of these dynamics, one for men, the other for women.

Those who decided to "stay little" in this stage may need to reestablish a dependency relationship in which nurturing is not conditional on being passive. Reclaiming the ability to initiate when needing something, will significantly develop *Power of Being.*

Conclusion

We build our *Power of Being* in infancy when we initiate contact by crying to let the world know we need something. We learn to feel, to sense and to be alive with sensation. We delight in physical pleasure, a soft caress, a nurturing touch and the warmth of being held close to someone. We learn to create a bond of trust in which we know it is okay to be alive, to have what we need and to feel.

Each time we repeat Stage One we have new opportunities to develop our power by learning new levels of trust and sensuality, by finding new ways to take in what we need and by creating or renewing new bonds to sustain us. Each repetition is also an opportunity to finish tasks left undone in previous experiences of this stage.

How we handle Stage One tasks will influence all the other powers in the developmental cycle, because in Stage One we lay the foundation for future mastery. Learning now that it is okay for us to be here, to be touched and to be cared for is the groundwork for a successful future.

Stage Two: The Power of Doing

Knowledge must come through action.

Sophocles

Summary

This stage has particular significance for those who are:

- between six and eighteen months of age
- age 13½, 26½, 39½, 52½, 65½, 78½
- age 19½, 38½, 57½, 76½, 95½
- after being nurtured for awhile
- in any new situation

51

- as a prelude to establishing a new level of independence
- as a part of a creative process
- in order to learn a new sensory skill such as music or language
- when taking care of a toddler
- in early puberty and ages which are multiples of them

Affirmations

It's okay for you to move out in the world, to explore, to feed your senses and be taken care of.

It's okay to explore and experiment.
You can do things and get support at the same time.
It's okay for you to initiate.
You can be curious and intuitive.
You can get attention or approval and still act the way you really feel.

Normal Symptoms

Symptoms can include wanting a variety of stimulation; needing to become grounded or to find a new footing; having tooth pain; being pleasure oriented; doing new things; having a short attention span; having motivation problems; wanting to see, hear, taste, touch, smell and move to explore the world and needing to expand the boundaries of life.

Deviations

Hurry Up. This means hurrying in doing things, being goal-directed instead of seeking needed pleasure, having high motivation to do things independently and using anger and goals to keep distance from others.

Stay Little. This means acting dependent and needy instead of exploring, adapting to others by doing tricks for attention, having a high motivation to stay dependent and not initiate, doing things inconsistent with needs to get attention, using fear and not doing things to keep others close.

Developing The Power Of Doing

Many of us were taught that exploring is only for toddlers. However, the need to explore occurs periodically throughout life. Being active and initiating each time we revisit Stage Two is how we develop our power to do things. We find out about the world through our senses of taste, touch, smell, sight, hearing and movement. This is the time to develop motivation, because we're naturally curious and intuitive now and ready to find enjoyment. This is the season to expand our options for expression and for action.

Brian

As an example, Brian Bentley is a grey haired man who is usually practical, businesslike and efficient. "But," he remarked, "I've been starting a lot of projects I don't bother finishing. I keep putting off anything that involves thinking. For instance, last week I got the urge to do some carpentry. I bought the wood and nails, even some new tools to make the job easier, but then I didn't start the project! Last week I started another project and then realized it was too complicated. I'm really resisting lists (planning things) or appointments. I want to be free to do whatever I want, not to be tied down.

"No matter where I'm going or what I'm doing, I really want to wear soft, baggy clothes that have a lot of room to move.

"Also, I get intensely involved in little things. I might point out little flowers or interesting pieces of rock. Some of my friends get pretty impatient. They're heading for the mountaintop and I'm fascinated by a pebble on the path! So I'm spending time with people who are willing to be patient.

"I like to go out but only when I know somebody will be there when I get back. The other day my son said that he'd be home when I got back and then changed his plans. That's usually okay, but this time I was really mad.

"Barbara (his wife) remarked about how easily distracted I am. She'll be all organized to get groceries or something and I'm fascinated by the color of the labels or the size of the peaches. And do I get irritated if she wants me to hurry up!

"Whenever I am somewhere new, I need to explore a little and get a sense of my surroundings before I settle down. Besides having fun, I find out things I wouldn't otherwise know, I'm more creative and I'm more efficient and more self-directed. Otherwise, I sabotage my work feeling confined and limited. I'll end up studying the form of a paper clip instead of doing my work. When I take the time to be indiscriminately interested in everything, going to the restaurant and studying the paper the menu is printed on and the crack in the table or the way the napkin is folded, I absorb what I need to turn my attention back to intellectual pursuits or conversation."

In Stage Two, issues predominate related to doing things: creativity, motivation, curiosity, intuition and locomotion. We may experience conflicts about whether to be passive or to initiate. Our dreams are often about movement, sights and sounds and are usually full of activity.

We need to find new footing or get our feet on the ground in a different way. Now we learn by doing, not by thinking. In fact, our attention span is greatly reduced. We may even have difficulty establishing or working toward goals because we want to follow our own urges without constraint. While we feed our senses, we want others to do the things that require thinking or concentration.

The feel for the world we gain in these explorations provides variety and interest, adds zest to life and contributes the raw materials — the sensory connection — to improve thinking in the stage that follows.

Each time we experience these symptoms, regardless of how old we are, we need to carry out the following tasks to develop our *Power of Doing:*

1. To explore the environment without having to think about it
2. To develop our sensory awareness and learn by doing
3. To taste, touch, smell, feel, hear and see what the world is about
4. To feel the earth, to find our footing, and to get in touch with the ground
5. To seek a variety of stimulation

6. To be free to move out into the world
7. To follow our own inner urges instead of what may be socially convenient or responsible

(Techniques for meeting these needs are listed in Part III, Chapter 5.)

Setting The Stage For The Power Of Doing

We carry out exploratory stage tasks for the first time when we're between six and eighteen months old. That's when we first become physically able to initiate not only by crying as infants do, but also by sitting up, scooting, then walking and talking. We learn about the world by tasting the dirt in the planter, touching and biting that heirloom vase, repeatedly dropping our toys, watching the moon, listening to birds and smelling flowers. We also develop a sixth or kinesthetic sense, the ability to move and sense movement.

To do this, we need continued bonding, support and affection while we learn about the world and get our feet on the ground. We need a continued abundance of food and touching to feel safe enough to explore. As long as we can return or tag in, touching base with our loving caretaker at will, we feel secure enough to move freely and satisfy our curiosity without having to inhibit our developing sensory appetite.

At this young age we're not able to selectively inhibit what we do. If our parents have to say no to something, we need them to provide a couple of yeses. They may say, "No, you can't play with the knife, but here is a spoon and a cup." Through these experiences, we develop an understanding of what's safe to do, or even *whether* it's safe to do things. We may ask, "Can I still get taken care of if I'm active and exploring?" The conclusion we reach to this major Stage Two question is a personal answer to whether or not we dare take risks, and how growing up will affect our ability to survive.

Cultural scripting affects exploratory babies so that they answer, "How am I supposed to feel?" and "How am I supposed to act?" instead of "How do I actually feel?" or "How do I want to act?" They are taught to engage in behaviors other people expect in order to get strokes. They learn that other people expect them to "act like a boy" or "act like a girl" rather than to "act how they feel" or "act on their needs".

Older people teach exploratory adaptations to infants through transactions. Mastery requires the ability to tolerate frustration, but people often hurry to aid a girl toddler who is frustrated. They soothe her immediately and may do it for her. Boys are often left frustrated for much longer so that they learn it's easier for them to give up asking for support than it is to try to get support. Therefore, girls learn to do by eliciting the aid of someone else, and boys learn to do by giving up support and doing it alone.

Because parents are usually inhibited by their own sex role scripts, they may want their children to express what their own scripting does not allow them to do. Thus, a boy child may be set up to express the aggressive urges of his mother and a girl child may be set up to express the passive urges of her father. A boy's desire to please mother may cause him to decide to become an achiever who sacrifices his needs. A girl's desire to please her father may cause her to decide to give up wanting to achieve in order to get what she needs. She may learn to take care of others if she is rewarded for "giving dolly a bottle" whereas the little boy masters aggressive traits. As a grown-up, he may be the "doer" out in the world and she may be the one who maintains the doer's supply lines by taking care of him.

We may decide, "I can explore the world and still be protected," "I have to give up being taken care of in order to explore," "I have to hurry up and start thinking because it's not safe to explore," "I have to stay little because there's no protection for me to explore," or "I have to do things that are inconsistent with my needs in order to get the attention I need."

We carry the decisions we make in the sensory and locomotor systems of our body, where they serve as the basis for organizing all behavior thereafter and automatically expand or limit our options for doing things. Our grown-up skills in meeting new people, learning a craft, reading and writing, enjoying our work, or even maintaining a pleasurable sex life are based on our Stage Two toddler experiences and conclusions.

Cycle Sabotage In Stage Two

When we "hurry up" through Stage Two, we often become agitated and rushed when doing things, as if we think that doing anything, no matter what, must be at the expense of pleasure or safety. We may have decided we need to "do, do, do" constantly in order to meet all our own needs, because there will be no support from others. When we "stay little," we may act dependent and needy instead of exploring; these actions are based on adapting to others. We inhibit our motivation to do things independently. We may have decided that doing things means abandonment; thus, we sacrifice support and do things anyway, or give up doing anything in order to keep others close.

Both deviations lead to sensory and behavioral problems. We may be overcome with fatigue at the thought of doing something, or find our motivation has evaporated into thin air. Or we may agree to do things and then back out, failing to understand that our fear of loss of support is driving us to constrict our actions and expressions.

Two other clues point to problems in Stage Two. One is competition in doing, as if only one person at a time can do something. The other is difficulty with issues related to food, money and sex. Although these symptoms are clues to the survival needs of Stage One, they are significant again in Stage Two because exploring the world creates new requirements for support. For example, one couple reported a scene that was becoming commonplace in their kitchen. It contained all the hallmarks of Stage Two problems, it related to food, to support and to competition about doing. One began preparing dinner; when the other started doing something too, the first stomped out angrily, saying, "When you're finished, let me know. Meanwhile, I'll get out of *your* way."

People caught in such dynamics may become senselessly adaptable, as if their very survival depended on doing only what the other person wants. One man stated that he kept needing his wife to do things for him although he was perfectly capable of doing them for himself. He said, "I noticed she was taking care of me, so I thought I should need to be taken care of!"

When people act as if they have to do things that are inconsistent with their needs in order to do anything at all, a dynamic referred to as "doing tricks for strokes", an exploratory stage problem is implicated. One woman described this in her relationship with her husband, "I used to take care of him and be tricky to get what I wanted rather than just *telling him* what I wanted. I'd feel sad, lonely and scared; then when that got to be too much to deal with, I'd just turn off my feelings completely so that I didn't have to do anything about it." We are often introduced to this as toddlers when required to do things that are inconsistent with the needs of an exploring baby.

We may maintain Stage Two problems by using a mechanism called projection. This is picturing what is in our own mind as if it is really caused by someone else. Couples are especially vulnerable to projection on each other; as long as one believes it's the other's problem, and vice versa, both are protected from doing anything about it. The doing is what brings up the fear of abandonment, punishment or loss of support.

If we lack the outer support for doing developmental tasks as toddlers, as adults we lack the inner support of having carried out these tasks in childhood.

Stage Two Games[18]

When we project our need to explore onto others, we play games (justify problems) instead of developing our *Power of Doing.*

We may experience others as being motivated, curious or talented, but grow passive when presented with opportunities to change or express ourselves. The following games[19] are typical of (but not limited to) this second stage of development:

1. **Harried** is often played by people who got attention only as a reward for doing things and not just for being. They're afraid if they stop doing things no one will ever notice them again.

   (For example, one person described playing *Harried.* First, she felt scared without knowing why. "I do things fast and don't always do them very well, but I get them done. I get real strong, and withdraw from people even if they're willing to give me support. I avoid them, I stay home, I don't want to go out of the house, and if I do, I look terrible. I eat a lot. I feel confused and mixed up and think if I could only figure this out I'd be okay.")

2. **Do Me Something** is played by people who don't ask directly for what is needed, often because they decided it was dangerous to initiate when they were toddlers. Instead they wheedle, whine or act seductive until someone else notices and offers them something. Then the switch occurs, and the giver is frequently set up to look inadequate.

3. **Greenhouse** begins with someone announcing they're about to have a feeling with the same seriousness one would use to announce they were about to give birth. They extort every last ounce of stroking from others as they explore new situations. This desire often is related to problems in getting attention or being protected when they were toddlers.

4. **Me Too** players act unable to do anything alone. They wait until someone else says what they want and then they say "Me too," a problem related to having to explore without protection or to being prevented from exploring.

5. **Gee, You're Wonderful** is played by people who project their own capacities to do things, or to be motivated, curious and creative onto others whom they believe have all the insights and abilities to perform miraculous cures. They never notice how much they themselves put into making situations workable.

6. **Cavalier** is played by people who pleased their parents instead of acting on their need to explore. They maneuver to keep people close as a way of dealing with anxieties related to weaning.

The Body Language Of Doing

When we leave exploratory needs for movement and sensory stimulation unmet, we fail to develop our *Power to Do*. We don't feed our senses or stimulate our skeletal muscles and voluntary nervous system, and, we don't expand our range of behavior and learn about the world. Inhibiting exploratory development shows up in our stress mechanism[20]; this self-protective system sends a surge of adrenalin for extra energy when we're under stress. Our heart races; our breathing quickens; blood rushes to our muscles as we get ready to fight, flee or freeze. Energy is released from our liver and broken down into sugar. Our pancreas sends a big dose of insulin to convert the sugar into energy for our muscles. Exploratory problems are linked to this stress mechanism because behaviors, such as freezing, fleeing or fighting, are linked to it. Stress-related diseases, such as heart attacks, strokes or sugar metabolism disturbances, are often rooted in the exploratory stage.

Some perceptual difficulties — speech, hearing and visual problems — are also connected to this stage. One person depended primarily on his sense of vision. He couldn't identify a taste unless he saw it first. He stumbled in the dark because he used his eyes to balance. He became phobic on carnival rides where he couldn't focus his eyes to orient himself. He hadn't been able to develop these senses during his exploratory stage because he'd been kept in a playpen.

A woman with exploratory stage problems was troubled by allergies. She said, "I'm furious. I've been told I have to start a four-year shot program for treatment. I have the hunch that this is a replay of something that happened before. It seems so familiar." In talking about how her exploratory stage was set, she discovered an important connection as a toddler; when she became angry, people responded with some intrusive skin stimulation, such as spanking, poking or tickling, instead of gentle touch. It was also during her first exploratory stage that she developed infantile eczema; she had been allergic since then. Her body was continuing to react as if all of life were a foreign protein against which she must defend.

You may have some untapped power potential to develop in Stage Two: (1) if you act as if someone said, "Don't bother," "Don't initiate," "Don't do things," "Don't be curious," "Don't be real," or "Don't be intuitive," or (2) if "No motivation," "Having to perform," or "Trouble doing things," are recurrent themes for you.

Reclaiming The Power Of Doing

In Stage Two we give birth to our ability to do or act, a faculty indispensible to attaining anything in life. In this section, people who were sabotaging their actions describe how they restored their capacity to do things. First they used Stage Two affirmations as seeds of power. Second they established deep nurturing ties to sustain them while they completed sequences of development they were not able to finish when they were six to eighteen months old. Finally, they worked directly with the sensory, perceptive and locomotor systems of their bodies. Of the following four people, two deviated from Stage Two tasks by "hurrying up and growing up". The other two attempted to "stay little".

Katie

Katie G. is a tall and slender, strikingly attractive and stylish blond woman of 38. Originally from California, she has lived in San Francisco since 1970. "I've been married twice and divorced since 1970," she said. "My first husband was very insecure about our relationship and very jealous. At first I loved being the sole center of his attention, but he tried to narrow down my world. My second husband I really cared about very much. But he was very attached to his father and he scapegoated me a lot."

Katie describes herself, "I am optimistic, have a good disposition, am overly timid, am not very assertive, am too eager to please other people, even when my heart's not in it." (Her adapting to others is a Stage Two clue.) She further states, "In recent years, I've had a lack of joy and outright dissatisfaction with my job. I'm getting older, with all that implies, and I feel scared. I'm not married and I haven't had a child. In fact, sometimes I feel that I don't have any of the things I want. I bought all the conceptions society has about age, lock, stock and barrel. Getting older really seems awful. I'm scared of entering this period of my life without having some other kind of satisfaction."

Fear has been a big motivator for Katie all her life. She says, "I fear that I won't meet somebody's expectations, or fear that there'll be consequences to pay for I don't know what, fear that people would find out I'm not competent, just FEAR. I'm scared to take risks, and so I hang on to what I've got. (Fear of doing anything is another Stage Two clue.) Having to go through so much difficulty any time I want to make a change is really torture."

To gain the willingness to take risks instead of keeping her world limited, Katie decided to recapture and regain the feeling of doing something meaningful. She dreamed, "Only one small light was on in my house, barely enough to see with, very limiting. Then there was a master switch that roared and the big noise scared me. My dilemma was to settle for the meager amount of light already available to me or to take a chance with the roaring switch, which could fill the house with light."

She confirmed the association of this roaring light switch with giving up her *Power to Do*. She continued, "I'd been to the bank before a session (with me) in March. I was feeling upset about money and trapped in a box." (Here I invited her to play in the box, an exercise designed to appeal to her exploratory urges.) Here she discovered, "I feel like I'm always sitting inside a box with not enough resources. I narrow my perceptions to the box and I don't see what there is to work with out in the world because I'm so busy coping with the box. I know when I was a kid there were playpens in the house and I was probably put in one.

"I remember my mom always giving me the impression that it was dangerous to go beyond a certain point. On outings at the park or at the beach, she'd be standing rooted next to the car, and even if I was far away from the edge of the beach or cliff, she'd yell out 'Be careful, don't go too far!' "

Katie's pattern of exploring in her adult life was to explore some possibilities, such as ideas for a new business, and then to end up not doing anything about them. She remembered, "I was exploring but I didn't have enough support. After awhile I didn't bother in the first place because I knew I'd run out of steam."

Even though Katie had defined her pattern clearly, like most people beginning Stage Two, she didn't know what she wanted to change. Instead of telling herself, "It's okay to explore and experiment," she berated herself for not knowing, "I didn't know what my goal was when I started." She needed to hear and decide, "It's okay not to make decisions; it's enough to explore your environment. It's even okay to be frivolous. You don't have to think about it yet; you can just explore."

At first Katie wanted to explore by talking. Gradually she expanded her abilities to include physical explorations as well. "If I felt something that was hard to think about, hard to express or put in words, I'd draw it with colored crayons. One time I drew a barrier. I'd never explored that way before. I couldn't draw at all, I thought. I found that doing physical things is important, such as punching the punching bag when I'm angry, having so much tension in my arms and being able to let it all out physically." Katie was also experiencing some tooth pain, just like toddlers cutting their first teeth.

At first Katie felt as if her feet weren't on the ground and she was out of contact. "Having someone to be sensitive with me, getting little, playing with toys and being held helped me decide to open up," she stated. She also tested to find out whether there were any conditions of support when she confided she was having an affair. She admitted, "I was afraid to say it for fear of being abandoned; I couldn't explore if I felt no one was available."

These experiences all were part of building a new foundation for exploring with support. Katie affirmed, "To make the transformation to the position that I can get support for exploring, I had to be willing to take the chance to ask and face the consequences whether I liked them or not. With support, I'm willing to tackle the risks. You have to dive the first time, but it's easier if you've got somebody you can talk with, whatever the consequences.

"What I'm doing differently now is seeing to it that I have support, like buying property. For the first time in my life *ever,* I've asked my parents for some financial support. And I'm looking at the possibility of shifting my whole economic base into sales. Also, I'm going slowly, not hurrying. I have more stick-to-it-iveness and I'm more assertive. I asked for a raise and got promoted on my job."

Abigail

Abigail H., a small pretty woman with curls piled on top of her head, had married her first boss on her first job after secretarial school. He'd admired her efficiency and had taken her out to dinner to show his gratitude; they'd been together ever since. For the last ten years, she'd used that efficiency in their home. Everything in their life was under control except one nagging symptom that wouldn't go away. She was working her way into an ulcer.

At first she responded to the diagnosis the same way she responded to all life; she got better organized. But the pain got worse. After nearly a year of trying special diets, and antacids but having continuing pain, Abbie took the advice of her doctor to find and change the "underlying stress factors".

Abbie joined with a small group of other people who were doing

similar work. At first she was eager to please, adapting at the slightest
hint when they wanted anything; she hurried and was busy without
much display of any emotion whatsoever, let alone pleasure. She
groped for answers when asked what she felt. In connection with her
ulcer, that feeling seemed to be only "cold and tense". She decided
to let that feeling take over completely and lead her where she
needed to go.

As she lay down with everyone around her, she began to breathe
in shallow little gulps of air. Gradually she began to fuss and turn
from side to side in tiny little movements like a feverish, delirious
baby. People picked her up, held and rocked her and gave her a
bottle of water. After about ten minutes, Abbie was cool and calm.

Slowly she began to talk, "I am a feverish, young baby in a hospital
bed. I am all alone; my mother is nowhere to be found. There are no
grown-ups around. I decide, 'There is nothing I can do to take care
of myself or motivate my mother to love me.' "

Instead of carrying out the developmental tasks of a toddler by
exploring the world and developing at her own pace, she had
comforted herself by organizing the world around her. Her inner
feelings and outward behavior were separated by a chasm of despair
and grief over the loss of her mother when she was sick and most
needed her. She'd pushed herself into a thinking stage before she
was developmentally ready, in an attempt to figure out what she
could do to survive and to get her mother back. Whenever she
attempted to bridge this chasm in her grown-up life, she reexpe-
rienced the same progression of events that included tension
building, building, building and then sickness following.

"Getting support" and "having feelings" were concepts without
apparent connection to that young inner Abigail who was too little to
understand them. Her *Do Me Something* game was motivated by that
young inner self who wanted her mother to come take care of her.
When people in the group showed motivation to love and support
her even at younger ages if she needed it, Abigail was ready to
change her decision and finish her exploratory development.

Abbie arranged to carry out some toddler developmental tasks at a
later session. She described the room, "Sharp objects were out of the
way. There were lots of safe toys, and a bottle and blanket. The others
held onto my watch and rings, my belt and my shoes so that my body
wasn't constricted. I agreed to stop being young if they asked me to.

We agreed I'd be able to stay young a couple of hours and leave 45 minutes afterwards to talk. Sam and Christie, friends of mine, were asked to have a couple toys ready in case I got into something they'd need to distract me from.

"I felt silly when they said, 'We're ready. Go ahead.' 'I can't,' I whined, 'I don't know how to do it.' I thought they'd hate me, but they rolled a tennis ball in my direction and I became fascinated with it. Then I heard a thump-thump noise. Across the room lay a golden brown heap of fur, and one end of it was going wag, wag, wag. I never thought to call it a dog or be aware it might bite. I made a beeline for it and caught the part that moved on the first try. I rolled my full weight onto the furry belly and pulled the wagging part into my mouth. Yelp! I heard, and my pillow started to move. They took my hand away and I was irate! Every part of my body, every cell and pore got behind screaming. I had been *wronged.* Somewhere in the din I heard another sound! Clack, clack, clack. Someone was banging two honey-colored wood things — blocks — together. I crawled over and we built towers and I knocked them over; then I spied a familiar blue thing with milk in it. I crawled to it, then back to my 'mom's' lap where I curled up, exhausted and thirsty. They gave me a bottle, put a soft blanket over me and that was the last I knew until I woke up.

"I am amazed to rediscover how anger feels. Once being young, I expressed total rage without a moment's hesitation or a flash of fear. The moment I had another option to explore, my anger evaporated into thin air. I am astounded by the contrast between those vivid experiences and the dullness of my day to day experiences."

Abigail continued to catch up on her development by feeding her senses. She had little desire to concentrate on long-term goals and wanted reassurance that she'd regain her concentration again. She mentioned that her sense of smell had not been operative but was now returning. She liked to chew things and said that her teeth were sensitive again, just like a teething baby.

Although Abigail needed more than a few weeks to catch up on a lifetime of development, she didn't need to stay in group all that time. Exploring the world is a lifetime proposition, and soon she was ready to leave that 'dull old group' to discover what the rest of the world had in store.

Bill

Bill T., an auto mechanic, was asked to describe himself. He chose what he believed his wife would say, "A willing worker who doesn't say what's on his mind." Bill then reported, "My boss is a guy who wants 80 hours in 40." (See Part I, Chapter 2 for an elaboration of his script and marriage partners.)

In describing a pattern he wanted to change, Bill also reported playing *Do Me Something.* He admitted, "A basic problem I have is letting another person do it for me rather than doing it myself. When something comes up, my first reaction has been, 'How can I get this done without doing it myself?' " Bill, too, experienced problems adapting. He'd been fine when he was alone, he said. "That is, I did what I wanted to do without asking anybody, and suddenly in my relationship with Marcia I found myself doing everything she wanted to do and none of what I wanted to do.

"Right now I feel I'm not getting what I need. My first reaction is that I can't do what I want because of her. But it's not her responsibility, it's mine. (Again the theme of doing and the mechanism of projecting the problem onto another are characteristics of Stage Two.) I was dealing with the symptoms through alcohol. Drinking to the point where I thought I was in better shape.

"In the last year I've probably had more problems with my asthma than in the last 30 years. I really get wheezy. I know that this is some basic thing I've been wanting from my parents for a long time. I don't have any recall, but I have this intense fear. You know how sometimes you leave your child in the car and go into the store? Well, that happend to me before I was old enough to remember. Also if I shut my eyes for a few minutes, a scene comes into my head. I'm in a hospital bed, looking through the slats in a very dark room. My impression is that both my parents are there but I can't get to them."

Bill found that "something" he wanted from his parents for a long time. He related, ". . . the most memorable night, one of the milestones, was when I asked you to hold me and I took a bottle. It showed me how simple it was to ask for what I wanted. I came in and got what I wanted. Up until that time I thought I had to do tricks. I knew at that point I didn't have to perform. There's no strings attached."

In freeing himself from feeling obliged to perform, Bill believes, "The major accomplishment has been opening myself up to my own needs and the fact that everybody has needs and that it's okay to ask for them. I'm more tranquil. If something upsets me, it's okay for me to say what I'm feeling rather than dump it on somebody else or look for the answer in a whiskey bottle. Little by little, I'm having more respect for myself and more for other people."

Michael

Michael G. is 53 years old, but he still has a toddler body due to a big pot belly and the outline of baby fat on his husky frame. He says, "It's a good thing I have a desk job, because I sure am accident prone!" Several months ago he fell off a ladder while painting his house and broke his leg. The year before that he broke his arm when he fell on his way to the car. In a recent group meeting he accidentally lost his balance, almost falling on Abigail. Then he sobbed, "I've been so upset this week but I've been trying to hide it. My eating has gone crazy; I've gained five pounds in the last three days. After last week's meeting I wanted to chew on something like a dog does on a bone. I took a bubble bath and ate popcorn at the same time. I thought I must be really angry to want to bite like that."

As he let that feeling take over, his back slowly curved and he began rocking, giving the impression of a baby learning to sit up. He drooled, then bounced a little, but never left his seated position even though some toys were within crawling range and people encouraged him to play if he wanted to. Soon he reported this scene. "I am young, very young. My father is never around. I want to crawl and see the world, but I dare not leave my mother's side. I can be little and she will hold me, but if I want to push away from her, I lose everything. I'm scared I'll be rejected if I grow up. I decide to stay little and stay safe. My first reaction under stress is to stop thinking and get people to take care of me. No wonder I've been clinging to women so tenaciously, being ready to promise anything or doing anything. I want to grow up and not be abandoned!"

Michael often did not hear what people said because frequently he was being younger than the ability to discriminate words. This not only had contributed to his accidents and earned him a reputation as a dummy and a daydreamer in grade school, but also was preventing his having rewarding friendships as an adult.

In the next meeting Michael explored hesitantly at first, but as he built confidence, he ventured farther and farther away from me. His caretaker lay on the floor and Michael crawled all over him; then, bored with being stroked and intrigued by a box of teething biscuits or a brightly colored bouncy ball, he headed off to see what he could see. He played for half an hour and then curled up to rest.

Michael needed to have new experiences in doing things *with protection*. With these experiences he could gain the body knowledge that each situation brings its own power and rewards. He had believed that doing things required huge effort; he saw his own abilities as almost nonexistent by comparison, as if he had to scale or crush a huge cement wall before he could approach the task at hand.

In the six months after he'd begun carrying out his exploratory developmental tasks, Michael lost 42 pounds and gained an appearance of length. By recovering his power potential in the exploratory stage, he had increased his vitality and his creativity. He says that he feels free of his accident problem. In addition, he decided to start his own business. "I was happy enough being at my old job," he said, "but I decided it was time; after all, that's part of being grown-up!"

Even when we're ready to explore, by continuing the physical affection that helped us develop our *Power to Be*, we also give ourselves the support we need to learn about the world by tasting, touching, smelling, hearing and seeing. As we develop our *Power to Do* (to act) by exploring, we create a wealth of sensory information about the world. This sensual and perceptual information is an essential bridge between Being and Thinking in Stage Three.

> *We shall not cease from exploration*
> *And the end of all our exploring*
> *Will be to arrive at where we started*
> *And know the place for the first time.*
>
>   *T.S. Eliot*

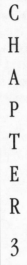

Stage Three: The Power Of Thinking

The whole of science is nothing more than a refinement of everyday thinking.

Albert Einstein

Summary

This stage has particular significance for those who are:

- between eighteen months to three years of age
- when taking care of a two-year-old
- when breaking out of a dependency relationship

- when developing new thinking abilities or learning new information
- when developing a new personal position or taking a stand on an issue
- when changing agreements with others
- at age 14 and ages that are multiples of 14

Affirmations

It's okay for you to push and test, to find out limits, to say no and become separate from me.

You can think for yourself . . . you don't have to take care of other people by thinking for them.

You don't have to be uncertain; you can be sure about what you need.

You can think about your feelings and you can feel about your thinking.

You can let people know when you feel angry.

I'm glad you're growing up!

Normal Symptoms

Symptoms can include asserting no and "I won't"; wanting to be different from others, especially if they were a source of nurturing; having tantrums; rebelling; complying; being temporarily forgetful or greedy; feeling angry for no reason; pushing others; developing a separate position and learning new thinking.

Deviations

Hurry Up. This means resisting feeling, refusing to think when scared, staying separate to avoid dependence, acting powerful and demanding instead of dealing with feelings or needs and attempting to control events.

Stay Little. This means acting agreeable instead of resisting, refusing to think when angry, staying dependent to avoid separation, acting charming or cute instead of thinking and often being controlled by events.

Developing The Power Of Thinking

In Stage Three we're ready to become independent individuals in our own right. The safe, warm security of dependency on others is rapidly becoming boring. We want to begin using the information we've gleaned from these experiences and to use our mind rationally. We want to find reasons for events, form our own conclusions and delve into the wonderful world of ideas. We want to become thinking people.

To do this we cross up our former dependency-relating to become separate from others, because thinking is a solitary activity. We establish boundaries between ourselves and others. We test them to draw the line. Testing activity is designed to establish, "What is and is not under my control?" or "Can I make something (or somebody) go away by pretending they don't exist?" or "Can I still get what I need if I think for myself?" Testing behavior of any variety crosses up dependency-relating, invites limits from others by pushing them and creates the space for thinking.

David

David H. is a bright, energetic young man of 28. He has done very well working for a computer company since graduating from college, but now he's feeling stuck. "This job was perfect for me then," he complained, "but now I can't imagine how I could have thought so. There's no room to be *me* here. There's just company rules, company policy and the *traditions*, the sacred traditions, sitting everywhere like stuffy old grandfathers. I don't know if I'll be able to keep this job any longer — or if I want to! I want to be a person in my own right, not somebody that fits into their mold! Maybe it's time I struck out on my own."

Sarah

"I know I'm beginning to separate because I'm repeatedly finding things wrong." Sarah D., an educator now age 54, was experiencing the negativity that is characteristic of Stage Three. An attractive, magnetic, dignified person, she began reporting fits of fussing. "I've even reminded my family to let me fuss instead of trying to take care of me or figuring out how to fix it. I can figure out what I need to do.

"Sometimes it's okay with me when the house is a mess; in fact, I like to be messy at home sometimes. Lately, I've been so preoccupied with it! Is the house clean, is it dirty, is this house mine, is this mess mine? I want to establish what is *mine*. I even love the sound of that word . . . mine!

"I've started gardening again. Even though a voice in my head says, 'Go do what you're supposed to do,' I just say, 'Not now, I'm working with my plants.' But really, I'm playing in the dirt!

"I'd been thinking so much about my husband and kids that I hadn't left any time to think about *me*. I was getting really angry and we were pushing each other. Still, I think they're happy I'm learning to say no. I even said it to the big kids at work — the bosses and experts! I fussed about a new policy for days. I told one of the chiefs I thought it was wrong and ended up getting thanked for it. I loved that! I want a whole new level of control and independence in my life, and I decided to push and find out how important I am to them. I feel so good exerting my opinion!"

Each time we return to Stage Three we begin a new level of testing activity. We may become preoccupied with finding or establishing our importance in relation to other people. We want to find the limits in situations. For example, how far is far enough, or too far? Where do I stop and you begin? What do I control in myself, this situation or this relationship? Wanting what's "mine" apart from "yours'" is a signal that a new level of thinking and individuality is bursting forth. As part of that process, we may invite others to think for us, and then become furious if they do.

Stage Three brings up separateness, responsibility and thinking issues. Resistance, compliance and rebellion, as well as contrariness and control become common themes around which our life revolves. As we learn to depend less on others and more on ourselves, we may experience bouts of forgetfulness, stubbornness, procrastination or greed. We may dream of being stuck, as if our feet are planted in mud and we're struggling to get free or panicking in quicksand.

Refusing to take things into account, or discounting, is a hallmark of this stage. For example, "What is your father like?" may be answered, "Yes, I was just thinking of him the other day at the store. Oh, and did I tell you I met Mary at the same store? She just happened to come by, and . . . ." Such an endless nonanswer is an expression of a person growing as an individual, who refuses to comply and who tests by not answering and not saying so.

The following are other examples:

Question	Discounting	Possible Answer
What time is it?	What's your hurry?	I don't know. *Or* it's three o'clock.
Did you do the dishes?	Oh, they don't have to be done until later.	No, I'm going to do them later.
What are you feeling?	I think the problem is the tone of my voice.	I feel scared.
You sound angry. Are you angry?	I'm disappointed.	Yes, I'm angry. *Or* no, I'm just not sure what to do.

Each further step into independent thinking may be marked by a series of discounting transactions: testing phases that are a prerequisite to separating and increasing independence.

Feeling angry is typical during this stage of development. The anger generated here is called *separation anger* because it is a tool used to break out of dependency. Temper tantrums are one form; some adults kick and scream, throw things or make messes just like children. Sometimes we report being angry with no apparent cause. Separation anger helps us create boundaries between each other. Once that purpose is served, resolving the anger is necessary. Instead we merely let it go just as we would let go of a shovel or a spoon after finishing with them.

Stage Three separation anger is different from anger that arises from needs not being met. For example, a baby who cries from hunger becomes angry when not fed. This kind of anger is resolved through expressing it, demanding what is needed and getting the need met. A second kind of anger is often called "paranoid anger" because the anger is a cover for fear. When fear is what motivates the anger, we need to feel safe enough to give up the anger and deal with the fear. When we feel separation anger we need to use the angry energy as fuel to motivate us to *think*. Thinking about how to take care of ourselves is essential, even though when angry we may feel a great temptation to sink into not thinking and saying, "I don't care."

Each time we begin Stage Three, we need to do the following tasks in order to develop our *Power of Thinking:*

1. Find out our importance in relation to others
2. Develop our concepts, take in information and learn to think
3. Find our own limits and those of the world
4. Make connections between sensory events
5. Express negativity and ambivalence
6. Push against others
7. Develop control
8. Have what's mine apart from you and yours
9. Establish independence
10. Exert our opinion
11. Test reality
12. Push against others

(Techniques for meeting Stage Three needs are listed in Part III, Chapter 6.)

Setting The Stage For The Power Of Thinking

The first time we begin to actively push and test those with whom we've been bonded as infants and toddlers we are between 18 months and three years old. We're often demanding, have temper tantrums and say no. Even though we want to stay connected, we're establishing that we're a separate individual. We want to develop control of ourselves and think for ourselves. We're finding out if it's safe to be separate and safe to think.

As two-year-olds we need limits within which we can safely test. It's as if we're saying, "I'm going to push you to let me go out in the street or eat too much candy, *but I want you to limit my doing it.*" We need our parents and caretakers to provide the structures within which we can make our first social contract, an agreement to temper our own behavior in order to get along with others and take care of ourselves. To establish these boundaries we test to learn, "Do I have to recognize you and what you want?" or "If I refuse to think about something, can I make it go away?" or "Will you still love me if I think for myself?" and "Will you still help me stay safe if I become an individual in my own right?" We learn to think independently and remember things at will. While learning whether or not and how to control ourselves, we may have bouts of constipation or diarrhea.

During Stage Three we still need to maintain our *Power of Being* (through physical contact and nurturing) and our *Power of Doing* (by exploring the world and feeding our senses). In addition, we need to develop our ability to think and become independent by finding the *limits* or experiences that establish the boundaries of acceptable behavior and safety.

Sex role scripting subtly influences how, when and what people think about. Generally, girls perceive the female sex role to encourage intuitive thinking, and boys perceive the male sex role to encourage rational and logical thinking. Thus, girls may decide to rely on instincts rather than logic, whereas boys in the same stage may decide to rely on logic. Because an air of fragility and less physical strength is associated with the female sex role, girls often keep their urges to push and pull and keep their strength hidden, as they sit still and play quietly.

Because an air of power and greater physical strength is associated with the male sex role, boys often emphasize their urges to push and pull and test their strength, as they noisily undertake rugged activities. The importance of girls' efforts to become separate is frequently diminished by their environment; thus, it may be easier for girls to stay symbiotic. Boys' efforts to become separate are often treated with more importance than necessary by their environment. Therefore, it may be difficult for boys to get dependency needs met. Girls are more frequently rewarded for tidy behavior whereas boys may be allowed to make messes without loss of stroking. Girls may be encouraged to stay dependent and use their thinking capacities to take care of others; boys may be encouraged to become independent and use their thinking capacities to deal with the world outside the home. Girls become "smart enough to get a man"; boys become "smart enough to stay 'one-up' on other boys".

Experiences during this first separation stage become the basis for conclusions that will govern what kind of information we allow ourselves to know and to think about throughout life. We may conclude, "I can think for myself and still be loved," "I can think to take care of myself," "It's dangerous for me to be separate," "I can think to take care of my parents, but not myself," "It's okay for me to think, but not about, for example, anger or my own needs." At the ripe old age of two, we determine whether new levels of independence are a threat, a cause for celebration or something in between.

Cycle Sabotage In Stage Three

When we "hurry up" through this stage of developing independence, we may decide not to think about fear. Instead, we attempt to control the space around us, especially by taking a strong position and being opinionated. We may have sacrificed needs for connection and nurturing from the *Being* stage to become independent, deciding, "It's better to separate than to be dependent or to need anybody."

When we "stay little" we often act agreeable or charming instead of resisting or testing. We may not think when angry; instead we give up control of ourselves and the space around us. We often avoid having our own position or opinion, having decided that it's better to maintain our *Power of Being* and sacrifice our *Power of Thinking*.

In either pattern we fail to use our own thinking capacities in the service of our own feelings or needs. In the first pattern, we give up needs in favor of thinking. In the second, we give up thinking in favor of needs and feelings. Both dynamics lead to problems in saying no or "That's enough", and in making and carrying out decisions that affect how we feel. Instead of proceeding with the developmental work of Stage Three and moving through it, we remain stuck; perhaps we feel stubborn, confused and contrary, unable to get beyond saying, "I won't," or "I don't like it." We simply do not bring our power of reason to bear on our personal issues because we haven't done the developmental tasks that would make it simple.

Stage Three Games[21]

When we leave developmental tasks from Stage Three undone, we play games[22] (justify problems) instead of developing our *Power to Think* and be independent. The following games are typical of (but not limited to) this Third Stage of the cycle:

1. **Look What You Made Me Do** is played by people who didn't separate. Because they didn't establish boundaries between themselves and others, they still expect other people to be responsible for their behavior. What others do is seen as the reason they didn't act adequately or they let someone down.
2. **Schlemiel** is played by people who got stuck in testing activity. They make messes and then apologize, proving they don't have to abide by the social rules others obey because nobody can make them do it.
3. **Tidy-Didie** is a corollary to *Schlemiel.* Instead of making messes these people clean them up, thus proving what good little people they are.
4. **Stupid** is played by people who got stuck in refusing to think as a way of finding out what they can control. Unfortunately, they found out they could control their caretakers by acting ignorant and unable to think. They've been stuck with it ever since.
5. **Sunny Side Up** is played by people who mask the depression they feel from losing affection when they wanted to separate. They see everything positively and cheerfully, with rose-colored glasses and sometimes through a haze of alcohol or other drugs.
6. **Tell Me This** is played by people whose caretakers refused to support them for thinking. They get others to fill in their thoughts for them because they fear losing recognition if they really think for themselves.
7. **I'll Show Them** is played by people who got stuck in a rebellious position when they wanted to separate. They're always proving how right they are by manipulating others into trying to stop them from doing something. They get someone else to attempt to control their behavior and then show others how impotent they really are by refusing to be controlled.

Body Language Of Thinking

The resistance characteristic of this stage is often physically expressed by holding the breath, thus limiting the brain's oxygen supply and the ability to think. Some people also tighten or constrict their neck muscles where the head pivots on the spine, a mechanism which controls how or even whether sensory impulses reach the higher centers of the brain.

Many people experience disturbances in their assimilation or elimination of food. When working through developmental tasks from this stage, they may have diarrhea or constipation or both, a temporary situation, which subsides along with testing activity.

When the two-year-old inside a grown-up is convinced that separation into independence and thinking for oneself means not surviving, thinking becomes an activity to be avoided at all costs, instead of a power to be developed.

Such thinking disturbances[23] are:

overdetailing or breaking reality down into small details to avoid the whole picture

overgeneralizing or focusing on the large picture to avoid an unacceptable detail

obsessing or churning thoughts over and over to leave no space for a threatening feeling

incompleting or beginning thoughts and leaving them for someone else to finish

Usually we disturb our thinking process in direct proportion to the level of danger we experience in separating. Thinking disturbances are a control mechanism or a protective device used to cope with a potential danger.

You may want to develop some untapped power potential in Stage Three: (1) if you act as if someone said, "Don't think," "Don't separate from me," or "Don't be Angry," or (2) if "Don't want to," "I dare you," "Can't make me," "Feel resistant," and "Not sure," are recurrent themes for you.

Reclaiming The Power Of Thinking

In testing to find out we can develop our independence and still be loved, we each regain and develop our *Power of Thinking.*

Beatrice

Beatrice Bach, whom we met in Chapter 2, had not carried out the developmental tasks necessary to finish separating from her father whom she described as "very caustic, negative and controlling."

"In my background change is a problem. Sameness is held as a high ideal; the same family, the same location. My dad hasn't yet made his separation from his parents even though they're dead. My brother hasn't separated either. He's 43 and still tied to Mother and Dad.

"I felt that for me it was either going to be separation or suicide, and because getting separate wasn't all right, I tried suicide. The first time I attempted and failed, I covered it by calling it a drug reaction. But I think I was totally stuck in my dad's structure." Bea who seemed so "together", who occupied a prominent place in the church, and whose husband's electrical engineering job provided a good income, Bea, of all people, shocked her friends with this attempt.

Bea's problem becoming independent surfaced in college when she was one of seven chosen for a coveted student teaching assignment. Mornings she'd eat breakfast, then go upstairs and throw it all up. "I was scared spitless," she said. "I know I'm capable, but I'm not perfect and I felt I had to be perfect." Soon she came down with neck pain and bursitis in the right shoulder. The doctor said that it was from all that writing on the chalkboard. Bea realized her mom had the same problem. She figured they were both using food to stuff down their feelings about her dad's anger, so that it came out in their necks. Then, too, she struggled with depression.

When she was younger it wasn't bursitis, it was asthma. When the school bell rang, she began to wheeze and her mother would let her stay home. "I was an excellent student, but I was afraid to fail, not to be perfect, not to be accepted by Dad and his standards." In her early 30s she suffered from highs and lows, wanted to succeed and feared failure, felt she could conquer the world and could not feel confident enough to decide what to buy at the grocery store. Also she had bouts of constipation and then diarrhea.

"I think I was purging, needing to get it out to Dad and tell him I wanted to be my own person, even if he didn't like me." So she decided, "I'm not going to play this game any more. I finally made this hellish uproar and began separating. I started saying no to what I didn't want to do whether or not it was okay with others."

At a weekend workshop Bea continued the tasks necessary to reclaiming her *Power of Thinking*. "At first I was really stuck," she said. "I wanted someone to give me something to adapt to, to tell me, 'Now we're going to work in this stage, Bea, you fit there, go do this . . .' and no one did; they asked what I wanted to do.

"The second day I tried a little rowdy play with a couple of other two-year-olds (other grown-ups working out separation issues). I began to become aware that people weren't going to go away if I got rowdy. We threw blocks and took possession of other people's things, and the grown-ups set boundaries ('You can play together if you don't hurt each other. You can throw the blocks without hurting each other. Watch them bounce off these pillows, or look, here's a basket to throw them in.')"

At a second weekend Bea continued testing in a large room set up to be an optimum environment for eight grown-ups who were doing similar work.

Bea recalls, "I remember us going in there like a herd of elephants, — 'Oh boy, let me at it, I'm going to have fun and not let them keep me under control!' We grabbed a big glob of pink play dough. We fought over it, trying to put it in each other's hair and eyes. The grown-ups firmly but gently said, 'No, no hurting each other, no putting it in each other's eyes, but you can play with it, put water in it and sift it.' That was so important, not having to be stuck doing something wrong or not doing anything. It was like giving me new roads, building alternatives instead of just being stuck.

"Later someone else took my blanket, and I wanted *my* blanket. One of the grown-ups let me have another blanket, and showed me where the blankets were so I could have my pick. That's something I missed in childhood — having limits with alternatives. The first time around I had a lot of 'either/or' parenting: you either do it this way or you do it that way, but there's not any latitude or flexibility. My brother was rebellious, doing the opposite of what Mom and Dad wanted. I was the adaptive good girl. As a youngster, over and over I got the message, 'We're gonna have you be perfect'.

"Being two and testing limits allowed me to experiment by not thinking for everybody and seeing what happens. I've always been an organizer and structure giver, and now I'm freeing myself from thinking for other people. I'm deciding I can be my own person and do it my way; that doesn't mean I'm in disharmony with other people.

"In the play group I didn't give up being a kid in order to take care of all the grown-ups as I had done as a child. I even let the grown-ups deal with another kid who got scared and started to cry. I'd play, then flip into taking care of everybody else and then realize I could count on the grown-ups to do the job, so that I could stay a child and play.

"To have someone else set limits for me changed a feeling of insecurity I've had in my grown-up life so that now I can play instead of feeling insecure. Also, I made a bond that grew out of being a two-year-old with someone else (another grown-up). So, we benefited for our individual reasons and our relationship benefited too. When we were playing, the other workshop member said out of a clear blue sky, "Your mom's a poop." She said it several times, and I realized, that really fits! She *was* a 'poop' — copping out and I couldn't count on her. Come to think of it, she and my dad and brother sit in the bathroom a *long* time. That helped me draw a boundary between her poopiness and me."

Since that play group, people have remarked how much more relaxed Bea is. She's enjoying being alone — something she didn't like before. "I don't have to be connected to everybody else in order to feel good. I'm still well-organized, but I can change plans and not feel the sky's going to fall in. Also, I can crack a joke, make light of something serious or be spontaneous.

"I still go back to that picture — what the walls looked like, the size of the room, the colors, the people and the feel of the play dough. That picture is the connection I needed between my thinking and my feelings. That picture helps me be decisive, even challenge in such a way that I get support for it. Also, I've given up some of my need for my husband to be a constant model for me. Instead, I'm making my own contacts with people, and he supports me for it. This new foundation for thinking is a bridge for some creative work for me. My next step is, I may do my Master's thesis on it. I may finish my degree."

Brit

Brit H., 42 years old, was a hard-driving, chain-smoking woman. She began testing the limits as soon as she joined a group to quit smoking. Although she'd read the rules and agreed not to smoke during group, she began to light up at a meeting at the same time she was delivering a lecture. "Listen, honey," she said, "I've done a lotta living, and you can't teach me a thing about quitting. I've tried them all: classes, cutting down one a day, chewing gum, quitting cold turkey and even taken up knitting. Never helped a bit except I've got some real nice sweaters."

She still remembers how shocked she felt when everyone reminded her of the no smoking agreement. She said, "I know you showed me the rules (posted on the wall), but I swear I never saw 'no smoking' on it. At first I was furious but then I was scared. I thought, 'I'm going to have to tough this out, too, just like I've had to all my life . . .' Then everyone just got up from where they were sitting and moved so I was in the center. They reached out, touched me and didn't say a thing. I just said, 'I'm scared' over and over. I think that's the first time I'd ever said it, admitted it, wanted to say it." Brit was changing her decision to act angry instead of thinking about fear. Her forgetting or discounting the no smoking rule and being confronted and supported was a first step.

In order to finish her separation process, Brit first established a new dependency relationship to reclaim her *Power to Be and Do.* She needed first to decide, "It's okay to feel" and "It's okay to act the way you feel" before she decided, "It's okay to think about feelings." She still smokes occasionally, but "I've lost my motivation," she explained. "I'd been trying to feed and nurture myself. Now that I've filled up that bottomless pit, I seldom want a cigarette."

Bert

Bertram Samuelson didn't hurry through his separation like Brit. Instead he dragged his feet, craved closeness and stayed dependent. An affectionate man with a big friendly smile, he often wears shirts that drape his large frame in a haphazard fashion, due to missing buttons or being incorrectly buttoned. He loves to eat good food, but his sexual appetite was what brought him to a problem-solving group. "I've got a lot of girls who are friends, but no girlfriends," he complained.

At first Bertram put more energy into eating the cookies and lounging on the pillows than working. His face was often marked by cookie crumbs on his chin or by a piece of spittle at the corner of his mouth. His pat answer to most questions was, "I can't remember." When asked if he was willing to say, "I *won't* remember," he began talking fast, breathing rapidly and twisting the corner of a pillow, working himself into a frenzy. When I asked him what was going on, he finally admitted he was mad. "When you asked me what I wanted to do about being mad, I got so frightened I wanted to crawl under the pillows and hide! Then when asked if I wanted to let the anger out, express it somehow, you might as well have been talking Greek. I didn't comprehend your words, yet I knew that's exactly what I needed to do."

Bertram said that he equated being angry with being in danger. He didn't have any inkling that being angry could feel good or be safe. To find out he could be as angry as he wanted to be and still be safe and supported, he lay down on a thick mat, took off his rings, shoes and necktie and then loosened his belt. The rest of us gathered around and carefully held his arms and legs so that he could struggle against us. We all agreed to stop if anyone asked to make further adjustments for safety. "Go ahead, then, do what you need to do," we said. At first he hesitated, resisted and even claimed he didn't feel angry. Nobody believed him. Then he whined a little and began to kick and struggle, surprised that it felt good. For about ten minutes he raged, struggled, kicked and screamed. Then his expression changed. He started thoroughly enjoying getting clever, seeing if he could trick us into thinking he wasn't going to move, catching us off guard and struggling suddenly. All were signals that he was beginning to think as well as feel. Obviously pleased with his cleverness he smiled, "I can do anything, right?" We answered yes, reminding ourselves to pay attention because we knew he was up to something. "Ka-ptooey" . . . he laughed, spitting. We quickly reached for a washcloth to protect ourselves. In several more minutes he grew weary and began to settle down.

"When I got to that point, I felt so satisfied with myself," he said. "Every trace of fear about being angry was gone, except that I needed the reassurance I could still be taken care of and I didn't have to sacrifice being cared for in order to grow up," he admitted. "That's why I wanted you to hold me. When you did, I felt even more secure and was able to do some more thinking. I think I've been angry most of my life, but I didn't know it. When you insisted I could answer you, I began to *feel* mad. Nobody'd ever insisted I could be responsible before. My father was always gone — gone to work, gone away on business or gone somewhere. That left my mother and me; my mother was 'gone' too, only in an emotional way. Taking care of me was her purpose in life. She was so lonely and fragile; if I pushed her, she got terribly upset. I finally decided to give up wanting to be my own person instead of an extension of her; it was too traumatic to everybody. She felt better when I was dirty because she had to clean me up.

"I didn't learn to think for myself. I've been a real patsy because of that . . . somebody tells me I'm nice and the next minute they've moved into my house with three dogs and a rooster, cleaned out my refrigerator, and I just feel guilty that I'm not being a good enough host."

Bertram's pattern is like many who "stay little" rather than separate. At first they show little motivation or discomfort about their situation. They often invite others to be uncomfortable by drooling, acting ingratiating or sweet, looking messy, picking their nose or letting it drip, talking loudly, giggling constantly, etc. For example, Bertram took up a lot of space, made a lot of noise, ate a lot of food, used a lot of pillows and assumed it was others' nature to be hostile to him.

Bertram, like many people who need to separate, stayed in a "feed me" position and wanted to eat when he needed limits. "Pushing away from my parents was like trying to push away from a marshmallow," he said. "They didn't have a happy sex life and my staying little and dependent was a lot of their satisfaction."

Bertram had needed to have a temper tantrum ever since he was two and had put off doing it. Going out of control in group was part of his completing a developmental sequence from age two. He continued testing and practicing saying no as he developed his long dormant ability to take positions separate from others.

He also set up many reinforcements that it was okay for him to think. For example, when asked, "What do you need to do about problems?" instead of answering "Think about them," he often said that he didn't know and then smiled expectantly as if waiting for someone else to think for him and provide the answer. He needed others' refusals to encourage him to think. Also, he agreed to bring snacks and then didn't do it . . . a test of whether or not we expected him to take responsibility for his agreements. "I was amazed when you all wanted me to leave the group to go get them, and then bring them again next week," he said. "When none of you did it for me, that was as if you were saying that I didn't have to take care of you by not being responsible for my agreements. That and my going out of control were two big turning points. They gave me a way of saying no. Once I could say no, I could also decide to think and to control myself. In other words, it was safe to grow up."

Beatrice, Brit and Bertram each finished in their own unique styles the developmental tasks they'd left incomplete from age two. Still, each of them learned how to be separate through a process involving discounting, stubbornness, anger and testing limits.

C
H
A
P
T
E
R
4

Stage Four: The Power Of Identity

Talk of mysteries! Think of our life in nature . . . who are we?

Thoreau

Summary

This stage has particular significance for those who are:

- between three and six years old
- after creating new boundaries for thinking and independence
- when seeking a new relationship to our family, job, group or culture
- when carrying out a new role or preparing to learn a new skill

- when caring for preschool children
- at ages which are multiples of four and five
- at 15 and ages which are multiples

Affirmations

It's okay for you to have your own view of the world, to be who you are and to test your power.

You can be powerful and still have needs.

You don't have to act scary or sick or sad or mad to get taken care of.

It's okay for you to explore who you are.

It's important for you to find out what you're about.

It's okay to imagine things without being afraid you'll make them come true.

It's okay to find out the consequences of your own behavior.

Normal Symptoms

Symptoms can include: wondering, "Who am I?" asking many why questions; being preoccupied with power; having interest in gender differences; experiencing nightmares; developing sudden, nameless fears; having an urge to tell lies or steal (just to find out what happens); wanting to test power; experimenting with social relationships; deciding, "Who am I?" and finding out the consequences of actions.

Deviations

Hurry Up. This means converting fear into anger and nurturing needs into sexual needs, and heightening awareness.

Stay Little. This means converting anger into fear and sexual interest into nurturing, and diminishing awareness.

Developing The Power Of Identity

Each time we develop our *Power of Identity,* we take cues about who we are now from who we've been. The parts of our personal history from previous identity stages are often the earliest and easiest to recall because of the highly verbal style and the vividness of the world-creating and destroying imagination we know here. Whether we're children or grown-ups in Stage Four, we're saying the same thing, "I'm here as a new individual with my own power to affect this system, and I can use it how I choose! I will influence this system one way or another."

Bernice

Bernice Brotherton is ready for a new life. Her children are grown and her job is a dead end. She wants to go back to school, but she's concerned it might be a waste of money at her age, especially because her husband wants to spend it on traveling and other things they haven't been able to do. "I feel all churned up right now," she says. "I'm in the middle of some reorganization of myself. I had a dream in which I was moving pieces around on a board, busy, busy. Then a voice said, 'You're an important person and you don't have to do all this.' I realized, 'Oh, there's who I am, and then there's what I do . . . that's not the same thing! That's scary and exciting all at the same time.' "

Roger

Roger Ray had been driving a taxi to support himself. When at last he graduated from medical school, he found himself in the throes of an identity change. "I feel a general discontent and malaise about work, home and mate. I'm restless; I want a radical change in my everyday life, the rut. I want to go off in the world and not be bound by my home life. I started thinking I've married the wrong person and for better or worse, I've been feeling sexually attracted to other women. I'm beginning to see that these are symptoms of needing to look inside and figure out how I'm going to get satisfaction in life. I need to build something different from this emotional discontent rather than changing outside stuff. I'm doubtful of the unknown and the new is untested, so I'm insecure. I don't have my old props to fall back on, the old touchstones that tell me who I am. It's like I'm writing up a new personal job description saying what I am willing to do and what I'm not. I feel pressed inside to define myself according to what I feel and want and not according to how I think I should be for other people."

Meridith

Meridith Robinson needed to build a new identity when her husband decided to be a minister. "When he went into seminary, I had a new role, and I was scared. For one thing, I can't remember names. I had to go back to my original identity in order not to buckle under the pressure to be 'the minister's wife'. I went through yet another identity change when I became a grandmother."

Lorrie

Lorrie Casselton has worked all her life and has done so for others. "I knew how to be a mom or a nurse, but I didn't know how to be a Lorrie. That's what my last several years have been about. I needed to make decisions about who Lorrie was, instead of seeing myself as a super-mom or doer all the time. I even changed my (first) name back to what it was originally. I'm selling my house and giving away things I've had for 30 years. I thought that might be depressing, but what makes it exciting is that I'm choosing to do it. I don't have to carry all the clutter of 30 years in order to be Lorrie."

"Who am I?" "Who is this person called me?" "What are my likes and dislikes, my talents and allegiances, my heartbreaks and desires?" To answer such questions is to know who we are. To create an identity we test to find out what happens *if*: (1) I don't wear the right 'uniform' to work even though I have for years, (2) I decide on a new job or career, (3) I send the kids to camp and take a separate vacation or (4) I do or don't stick to my budget (or diet).

To test out who we are we find out what effect we have on the world. We may start a rumor or change from one style or social group to another. We may also become preoccupied with deciding what or who is crazy or sane and what is fantasy or reality. We may experience nightmares full of frightening monsters or surreal events or life-threatening situations.

We may become fascinated by characters in books, plays or stories, trying these images on and even using some to shape our definition of self. We may identify with a character in a myth, or a movie star, political figure, an older, admired acquaintance or even an animal. "I'm like a unicorn," one person explained, "because I'm an endangered species." Another said that he felt like the ugly duckling, not much to look at now but a beautiful swan inside.

We're likely to become fascinated with discovering the dynamics of relationships, finding our place in groups of people and determining how we can affect them. We may set up fights or conflicts to ascertain the extent of our influence and find out the consequences of our actions. We may even lavish attention on one person and barely notice another to see what happens.

We also may become preoccupied with what it means to be male or female, because identity is based on gender differences that are both cultural and biological. "I am a girl or woman, boy or man" is a biological fact, but what are the consequences of it? What does it mean in my life? As part of answering this question, we may become attracted to someone else's sexual partner. (Remember Oedipus, who killed his father and married his mother?) Each of us decides about what it means to be the sex we are and about our influence or authority in the world based on the results of our testing.

The results of our experiments are the basis for decisions. Dismantling an old identity and laying groundwork for the new takes time, because we are shedding an old skin and readying the new one.

Each time we revisit Stage Four we need to do the following developmental tasks to develop our *Power of Identity:*

1. Find out, "Who am I?"
2. Discover what being male or female means
3. Test definitions of reality through consequences
4. Exert power to affect relationships
5. Separate fantasy from reality
6. Develop the ability to organize and change our internal reality

(Exercises for dealing with these needs are listed in Part III, Chapter 7.)

Setting The Stage For The Power Of Identity

We first create an identity between three and six years of age when we play with the possibilities about who we are and who we can become. We begin by asking "why" questions. "Why is the sky blue?" "Why do our lips move when we talk?" "Why is Daddy a boy?" "Why am I me instead of you?" We are learning to create our own unique version of the world by manipulating images, experiences and concepts from the world we live in. We come into our own power as social individuals through testing and experimenting with how we can affect others.

We also take an active interest in differences between people, especially between males and females. We decide whether we are a boy or a girl, and what it means to be the sex we are.

As children we decide "Who I am" in sexual terms. We answer what it means to be a boy or girl in terms of basic okay-ness, getting needs met, dealing with feelings, having the ability to do things and having the ability to think. Being a boy may mean acting tough and scary, being able to take pain or dish it out, keeping a hard exterior as a way of dealing with feelings, being able to do things, thinking about how to win fights and not thinking about how to take care of self or others. It may mean deciding to act better, smarter and stronger than girls. It may be motivated by a castration fear. "I may have been born a boy but if I don't act like I've got balls, pretty soon *I won't* have any" is the four-year-old's logic.

Girls may decide being a girl means acting fragile and scared or being easily made uncomfortable like the princess in the story, "The Princess and The Pea". Girls may decide not to do things independently but to be the helper of others who are doing things. They may think about how to be coy, cute and pretty, and not think about how to deal with the larger world. Girls may decide never to appear smarter than men, to never trust men or to trust only men.

The identity we create here is a summary of all our experiences and decisions to date, beginning with Stage One when we experienced life as a sea of physical sensations and gained our first sense of what life was like. From Stage Two we include experiences in moving, sensing, smelling, tasting and touching: from Stage Three we add experiences, becoming independent and learning to think for ourselves. Information about *me* from other people is included along with what we learned from having our fantasies and testing the consequences of behavior.

The conclusions we reach here have an inner, personal function and an outer, social function. Inside, they act as the neurological communications center or switchboard that processes needs, feelings, behavior and thinking. In the social world they form the pattern for a statement of our place in the natural and social world.

Identity decisions in childhood determine our behavior and life course long after the four-year-old stage is a dim memory. For example, we may decide we want to be treated like a brother or sister who receives certain privileges or presents; thus we decide we're someone who always gets less than others. We may believe we have a quality or strength that is usually attributed to the opposite sex and decide we are not really the sex we are. This decision produces gender confusion. Because we will create in the following stage an entire technology of personal skills, such a decision may also lead to problems with sexual adequacy in later life.

Cycle Sabotage In Stage Four

When we "hurry up" through our identity stage, our sense of who we are may be solid and fixed because we avoided the testing necessary to create it. We may have identified ourselves as someone who doesn't have dependency needs, but rather prefers others to keep their distance. We may avoid feeling by thinking. In answering, "Who am I?" we may have left out the ability to nurture ourselves, because this capacity is built on the ability to feel. Lack of feeling emotional hunger, leaves us hurting, or acting powerful or omnipotent. To prevent feelings, especially fear, we may have identified ourselves as a person who makes sexual overtures when scared.

When we "stay little" in Stage Four, we may convert anger into fear or sexual feelings into nurturing or being nurtured by others. We may have identified ourselves as someone who is too scared to think. We may believe that independence means danger or assume that growing up means loss of contact. Instead of acting how we feel, we may do tricks that are inconsistent with our feelings to extort the affection we believe we can't get otherwise. We may become angry when physically active and may retreat into an inner secret garden rather than show others how adequate we can be. We may believe that other people are suffocating us, such as being strangled to death or ingested and swallowed up like Jonah and the whale. We may fear growth (if we were too confined to move freely by a playpen), a smothering relationship or constricting rules about what proper or good little girls or boys are. We may have nightmares in which we have insurmountable difficulty getting from one location to another in order to be safe.[24]

In contrast to the fear in the "hurry up" pattern, this fear is designed to deal with a world in which effective parenting is absent. Thus, we may have difficulty answering the question, "Scared of *what?*" because our fear is a nonspecific self-protective device.

When we "stay little," we may sexualize our anger. For example, one woman stared at others' genitals when she felt angry, whether at home, in the supermarket or in church. A man began to play with his genitals when angry. Both had concluded that two people could not need something at the same time, acting as if they were under orders not to need anything except from their parents.

When we believe that our own abilities are much larger or smaller than they are, we may have had an inappropriate power position in our family. For example, one man's role as a child was to stay in between his parents, constantly needing, wanting and being ministered to so as to keep his parents' attention on him rather than on some of the threatening problems between them. With the logic of a four-year-old he had decided that he could keep them together by being demanding.

When we create an identity that allows for only one fixed role rather than expanding options, we can realize only a small portion of our potential self.

Stage Four Games[25]

When we leave developmental tasks from Stage Four undone, we set the stage for playing games[26] (justifying problems) instead of developing our *Power of Identity.* The following games are typical of but not limited to this fourth stage of the cycle:

1. **Mine's Bigger Than Yours** is a gender testing mechanism for four-year-olds that becomes a game when used to cover and pass onto someone else a feeling of inadequacy.
2. **Let's You and Him Fight** is another normal developmental process that is turned into a game when used to garner attention. Initially one person sets up a fight between two others, and then becomes indispensable to their patching things up.
3. **Uproar** is played to avoid sexual intimacy; especially between family members where incest is taboo. Starting with a fight, it ends with a slamming door.
4. **Rapo** is played by people of both sexes who invite another to expect a certain something (sex, affection, ice cream or a present), and then pull a switch, leaving the other party stranded with their assumption and feeling stupid.
5. **Buzz Off Buster** is a variant of *Rapo* in which the other player is first seduced, then abandoned.
6. **Cops and Robbers** is played by people who do things they know are wrong and then get caught. They garner a great deal of negative attention while reinforcing the decision that they're no good and neither are the authorities.
7. **Let's Pull A Fast One On Joey** is played by two players who unite against a third. Once again, the theme is seduction and abandonment.

Body Language Of Identity

Physical problems related to Stage Four may include: problems with basal metabolic rate, the rate at which our bodies convert food to energy and our glands secrete hormones; problems with circulation, such as high or low blood pressure or headaches caused by circulatory changes; or chest pain, heart palpitations and disturbances in heart rhythm.

Heart symptoms may be related to caring for the heart as the center of lactation, nurturing and giving. People who created an identity that cut them off from caring may have heart pain and circulatory problems — symptoms of a broken heart. Other physical symptoms in this stage are specific to the identity we created.

You may have some untapped power potential to develop in Stage Four: (1) if you act as if someone said, "Don't be sane," "Don't be straight," "Don't be powerful," "Don't be loving," or "Eat your heart out," and (2) if "Don't know who I am," "But what happens if," or "But that's not me," if you feel powerless or often experience conflict between this and that (person, idea, lifestyle) are recurrent themes for you.

Reclaiming The Power Of Identity

The following case studies about Susan, Sally and Joe show how they for their own reasons and in their own way, reclaimed their right to the *Power of Identity*.[27]

Susan

When Susan B. was a little girl her life was fairly complex. She was the first child, so her mother had to learn on her. Then there were too many other babies too soon and too little support. Her mother turned to alcohol and Susan played Mommy when she needed to be a kid herself. When Susan was exactly three years and ten days old, she was taken from her mother. Susan concluded with logic typical of childhood that she was taken away *because* she'd been testing her power. If she hadn't been actively discovering who she was, this would never have happened. She decided then and there not to create her own identity. Susan remembers sitting in court, listening to all the awful, negative things the judge said about her mother. Susan took them on herself. After all, if her mother was bad, Susan was bad, too.

Susan was placed in a couple of foster homes before she was adopted into another family when she was five. She'd been split up from her brothers and sisters. The next youngest child after Susan (whose life Susan had saved earlier by pulling her from a burning building) failed to thrive until returned to live with Susan. She, too, was adopted by the same family. Susan decided she was responsible for her sister's life.

In the new family things went fairly well. Her new parents had insisted that the children they'd adopt have college potential. Susan tested out at the top 3% of her class, but her grades didn't show it, a fact which caused considerable displeasure at home. Also, she was sick about six weeks every fall with bronchitis, terrible sinus problems and bad headaches.

Whenever Susan spoke of finding her genetic mother, her adopted mother told her she was going to find trash. She said Susan's genetic mother had four faults that Susan, too, would have to worry about: being fertile, being promiscuous, being fat and being alcoholic. Susan worried about them all, even though she didn't know what they meant.

She also worried that she'd get taken away again. To prevent that, she steadfastly avoided her 'crime' at age four — she did not create a single, unified identity. "Instead, I felt like I had two personalities," she said, "one from the first years and the other from my adoptive years. When I did bad things and they said, 'Why did you do that,' I'd say I didn't do that. I'd shove it off on that other little girl that was the first years of my life. I'd say to myself, '*This* Susan would never do that because she would not want to hurt her mom and dad.' I did not want to get sent back."

Susan's new mother may not have understood, but she noticed. She said, "I don't know you from one day to the next; your personality changes all the time."

In high school Susan defended herself against the unknown dangers of her genetic heritage by avoiding boys or only going out in groups. When she turned 21 and took one drink, she thought, "That's it, I'm an alcoholic now." "Also, I did prove to be fertile, but I lost a lot of babies. Not knowing who I was, I was scared to death of what I was going to give birth *to!*"

Susan continued to worry and have miscarriages. When she was 26 she had what amounted to a nervous breakdown. Viewing this difficult time from the vantage of recycling theory, her difficulties at age 26 are easily accounted for, even predictable. Knowing her mother had difficulty coping right from the beginning, we easily guess that Susan did not get the full support she needed and no doubt left Stage One developmental tasks unfinished. At 26 her developmental clock and the birth of her first child triggered a natural recycling of Stage One. Added together, these ingredients result in an intense year of survival tasks, a natural opportunity to make great developments in the *Power of Being.*

She went to a psychiatrist who told her that she was having postpartum depression and that it would go away if she took a lot of pills. He gave her a six-month supply of three different tranquilizers. She counted them out; there were easily enough to kill herself and then some. Instead, she took them according to his instructions for a while and didn't feel anything. Then she decided she wanted to live.

"What I needed to do was move back and search for my genetic Mom." Her husband agreed, and they moved. "First I searched for my brother and sisters because that was more acceptable" (meaning less threatening). After seven years she found them. Then she helped organize a group to help other adopted people search. "I was incredibly successful," she reported. "I found genetic mothers by the score, and sometimes within half an hour."

At a workshop she attended Susan told a little bit about herself and her work. An astute person there said, "How come you haven't found yours?"

"I didn't have an answer, and I knew I'd have to come face to face with it, so I decided to find her. And I did, two weeks before my 30th birthday (also two weeks before her developmental clock began recycling age four).

"It was as if you'd taken a big heavy mystery that had always been in front of me and thrown it back over my shoulder. I turned around and looked at it and there was my past, right where it belonged instead of always being in front of everything. I could begin to know who I was. That gave me what I needed to look at myself. Up until that time, I wouldn't even look in the mirror. Now I could not only look, I could see I was pretty."

Finally she could construct an identity of her own. She was safe enough and she had the pieces of her past she needed. As an ultimate test, she summoned all her courage and asked her adopted mother her "big question". "If you could have just had Kathy (her sister) and not me, would you have sent me back?" The answer was immediate. "We never would have considered such a thing!" At 30 she finally felt she belonged to her family for the first time.

Susan began to reconstruct her *self.* First of all, she knew who she was in part by how she felt so that she began sharing her feelings with people. Next she moved, again because she needed to be close to her adoptive parents while she continued to assemble who she was. She also asked the community of people to which she belonged to point out when they saw her being the unique person she was . . . when she was spontaneous.

"At age 30 I didn't have the tools to build myself. I couldn't build on what happened when I was three and four. I was building on rotten stuff." In a few weekend workshops, Susan went back to being three and four to build a new foundation. "One time I was three, before I was taken away from my mother. I found out there was enough love for me by being particularly naughty and having people say, 'No, I love you, don't do that.' At one point a grown-up asked us to be quiet because there was a baby in the room; that was horrible . . . once again a baby was in the way of doing what I wanted. So all my friends (being three also) went under the table and built a fort. Everybody piled on top of me and I felt so smothered I thought I was going to die. One of the grown-ups said, 'You come out and we'll find something you can play with.' And it was like the whole thing had just been lifted off me." (She let go of the weight of always being responsible for the babies.)

For three weeks afterwards Susan's lungs and sinuses cleared tremendously. "Then I realized I was always sick in October, and that's when I was taken from my mother! I'd be sick on and off until February, which was my birthday! I haven't had bronchitis since I was 30 years old.

"I found out that I'm lovable and that I'm not responsible for my sister's life, just mine. And I'm okay the way I am; it was the situation that was out of my control." (Here she is giving up the grandiose sense of her own power she'd had since she was three.) "Also, I can think and feel, not one or the other." (In building new connections between feeling and thinking, she was building a new foundation for her identity during the workshop.)

And she learned, "I could start acknowledging myself. If I did something well or that felt good, I could say, 'Hey, Susan' because I know who Susan is. When somebody used to ask me to do something, I had felt cornered and never sure. Now when I take on a job, I know I'm going to finish it. Also, I didn't dare dream before because I didn't think a dream could come true. Now I have goals and dreams and I feel my feet are planted on the ground, where I want them to be. I know who I am!"

Susan's accomplishments are more than personal victories. In 1979 she received the Outstanding Young American Woman Award.

Sally

At age 52, Sally D. has developed her *Power of Identity* many times. Some phases had been smooth as silk, others a complete fiasco. An early one, leaving a small Nebraskan town to go to college 50 miles away was cause for celebration because it was what she wanted; she wanted a husband and college was where to find him. Also, she had maximum support. The sororities were there to teach young ladies, and to guide them in creating a ladylike identity. Sally wanted that, too.

Another desired development of her identity was becoming a Mrs. The birth of children is an identity crisis for many women, but not for Sally. "When I was little I decided I was born for two reasons, to be a wife and a mother. I'd have four kids, two boys and two girls, and I'd stop having kids when I was 30 and that's exactly what I did," she said.

One of her first big identity problems began when her kids were nearly grown-up and she started getting scared of the time when she wouldn't be a mother any more. Then, within a span of a year, her husband died of leukemia and her beautiful daughter was killed as she walked down a sidewalk by an out-of-control car.

"Part of me died, too, when she died, because part of my motherhood died." (Meaning her identity as the mother of her daughter.) "I thought, 'I'll never be a whole person again.' " With the help of supportive friends, she began to reconstruct herself. Slowly, the realization came that there were not only problems with who she was now, but there were also problems with who she had been and things she hadn't been aware of.

"For one thing I would lie," she said. "I had no qualms about it. I felt more frightened when I told the truth. Then, too, I'd get attracted to someone else's partner. That way I was safe. I didn't have to be intimate and yet I could be as sexy as I wanted to. If he initiated, that was his fault. I never got in trouble, luckily. I was going to get power by association." Then there was the gnawing sensation that something inside her wasn't getting what she wanted. Also, she was not a person to talk, and keeping quiet was of little advantage. Finally, she received evaluations from the students in a class she taught. All of them said that she was cold, distant and far away. "That was too much to ignore," she said. "I had to change." She had to face her internal belief about who she was. She said, "I did not believe I had enough power to get what I needed."

She began her change in a couple of unlikely ways. First, she was going to solve it and then she was going to get support. Luckily she quickly learned that was backwards. Also, she had an affair and, short lived as it was, it was the beginning of a new identity.

A little later she flew to California to attend a workshop recommended by a friend. To her surprise she spent most of the time crying uncontrollably. "That scared me enough to start taking responsibility for who I was," she said. To start breaking out of her secret, internal world, Sally started blaming out loud, instead of in her head. In so doing she realized that what she felt and what she thought were not together at all (a symptom relating to identity, which serves as the link between the two).

When Sally was first creating the foundation for her *Power of Identity* at four, her mother was ill for nine months and then her brother was born. "I didn't get the attention and care I deserved." Her father was gone most of the time, but she and her mother were befriended by the local doctor. "He was nice to me. I wanted him to come to the house because mother wanted it. She was nicer to me then. If I was sick, he'd come over; so every day I'd be sick . . . some kind of liver problem, they said. I took a little liver pill every day and would throw up and then the doctor would come to our house."

Sally recalled her mother reading her a story about a queen . . . a snow queen who lived in a big castle. The queen was cold and cruel, but she wanted children, and when she got what she wanted, then she was nice. Since I was being ignored so much I decided, 'I'll go and get myself a special place; then I'll be better and bigger and nicer than you. I'll be a queen, and then if I want strawberries for breakfast, I can have whatever I want.' "

Sally decided not to carry out some of the normal developmental tasks that kids her age do . . . she never asked "why" questions, for example. "I acted like I knew why. The sky was blue because it was painted blue, that's why."

In creating an identity that didn't include needs, Sally had laid the foundation for a symptom that had plagued her all her adult life.

She'd become completely incapacitated by sick, migraine-like headaches that would last for days. She began to understand how the headaches were her body's way of telling her she needed to develop her *Power of Being*. Using the pattern she created when she was four, when she needed caretaking, she got sick enough to send for the doctor! Until that time Sally had experienced herself, not as a whole person, but a fragmented series of hunks here and there. Her goal became "to get the hunks together".

At first she tried to throw the Snow Queen out completely, but there were parts she liked and wanted to keep, especially that exhilarating feeling of being tall and powerful. She wanted to be queenly but no longer aloof. She consciously changed her posture from an authoritarian pose to a relaxed, open one which invited intimacy. She decided to have fun teaching the queen to be mellow and loving to herself instead of being harsh and cruel.

To experience kindness and warmth toward herself, for 15 minutes a day Sally put on a pretty dress and ate from a pretty plate she usually saved for company. Soon she forgot to limit it to 15 minutes, and raised her own level of nurturing to herself in all areas of her life. Still, under stress she reverted back to the cold, aloof Snow Queen. To change that Sally created parts of a new identity foundation based on having needs and getting support instead of denying them. In the same play group as Susan, Sally, too, played under the table in the fort. When someone being two wanted to play, Sally responded, "No." She further related, "Some big person came and took the baby away and that was a wow . . . a message that it was okay for me to have my needs met too, something that wasn't okay when my brother was born."

A second part of the new foundation came in another play group. Most of the kids were enjoying play dough, but Sally noticed some soapy water in a laundry tub nearby. She was having a superb time splashing it all over everything when one of the grown-ups told her the water was dirty. Sally told her she was *wrong*. "That was an important turning point for me, knowing I could be right in the face of this authority." (Here she's deciding to have her own definition of reality, an essential task for four-year-olds.)

"After that I started standing up and verbalizing what I knew was right. Right now, that's leading to more problems in a way, because I'm not willing to ignore situations when I believe I'm right. Instead, I have to deal with it somehow, and I need to learn how.

"Also, having the man co-leading the group stay by me and not go away or be pushy was important. I saw that I didn't have to do anything special or tricky to get a man's attention. That's a new foundation for beginning to trust men. I see them in a different light now, like I felt when I was with him."

Although Sally wants to do more work to develop her identity, she has freed herself sufficiently to become interested in men again. This time she has her own power instead of wanting to borrow theirs, and she's finding those who are really available.

Joe

Joe Lagrabotti is a husky man with strong, thick forearms and biceps conditioned by lifting weights. In his middle 40s, he is successful by most standards. He lives with his wife and two boys in an affluent suburb. He works as an account executive with a major oil company and coaches Little League.

The rest of his life stood in sharp contrast to periodic episodes of violence. Most of his friends would get a little tipsy or sexy/friendly when they drank, but Joe got nasty. Once after friends had subdued him and taken him home, he'd beaten his young son, leaving physical bruises and emotional scars. Joe joined a weekly group reasoning that he needed to learn to control his temper.

He started by agreeing to tell people what he felt. Soon he identified a pattern, which was marked by an urge to become violent, preceded by his becoming afraid of a sexual overture from other men. "I was really scared at that point," he said. "I knew I had to get to work on it. I remember stating two things I wanted to do that were mutually exclusive and wanting people to tell me how to resolve the conflict, but instead they insisted I work it out for myself. To do that I had to go into my past."

The next week Joe reported a recurrent nightmare. By working with the dream, Joe soon recalled scenes from ages three to four in which he'd been shamed for feeling. "I decided feelings are for girls. Outwardly I tried to be a big boy and not feel, but inwardly I knew I must be a girl because I did have feelings and needs." Joe, the grown-up, was protecting Joe the little boy by doing something violent, a powerful way to regain control of a situation.

Joe began asking other men in group about their feelings, needs and experiences. An important turning point came when he sat next to the male co-leader, being held close, and asked questions he'd not asked when young the first time. "Do you like me? Are you scared of me? Do you like to hold me? Did your daddy hold you when you were little? Did he hold you when you were bigger? Are you going to hurt me? What will you do when you get mad at me?"

A few sessions after that he attended a play group, where he played in a sandpile with three other grown children being age "three to five". Testing the power of his new internalized Daddy was the object of his play. When all the "children" got in a rowdy discussion about throwing sand, Joe proffered proudly, "My daddy says you shouldn't throw sand!" When his buddy threw a shovel, Joe blurted out, "You scared me!"

After that Joe focused on how to's — such as how men deal with fear, how to relate to other men and still have feelings and how to meet his contact needs. These signaled that he was working in the next stage, learning new skills and changing parts of his value system.

To know who we are is a birthright we all have but may leave unclaimed or undeveloped for a variety of reasons. Our developmental cycle affords many opportunities throughout life to carry out tasks necessary for having a new, harmonious and effective identity.

<table>
<tr>
<td>
C
H
A
P
T
E
R
5
</td>
<td>

Stage Five: The Power Of Being Skillful

</td>
</tr>
</table>

For the things we have to learn before we can do them, we learn by doing them.

Aristotle

Summary

This stage has particular significance for those who are:

- between six and twelve years of age
- after changing identity decisions
- when learning a new way to do something
- when parenting a six- to twelve-year-old

- at ages which are multiples of six through twelve (multiples of ages eight through nine are especially significant)

Affirmations

It's okay for you to learn how to do things your own way, to have your own morals and methods.

> You don't have to suffer to get what you need.
> Trust your feelings to guide you.
> You can think before you make that your way.
> It's okay to disagree.
> You can do it your way.

Normal Symptoms

Symptoms can include preoccupation with "how to do it"; interest in others' values and morals; wanting to criticize others' ways; wanting to do it our own way and nobody else's; becoming literal and argumentative; arguing and hassling with others' morals and methods.

Deviations

Hurry Up. This means learning how to act grown-up and competent, how to hide feelings and how to be over-organized, discriminating and rigid.

Stay Little. This means learning how to act little and incompetent, how to hide thinking and how to be under-organized, indiscriminate and lax.

Developing The Power Of Being Skillful

When our developmental clock reaches Stage Five, we may reexperience the first four stages briefly. First, we prepare our being; next we do things to explore the world; then we test thinking, limits and boundaries; and finally adjust our identity before beginning to update our values and skills. At that point we may become literal and argumentative, like an eight-year-old lawyer. We may feel clumsy and awkward again, like a kid who's growing too fast to keep up with the size of her body. We may make frequent mistakes as we try out ways to make things work. Contact with people outside our usual circle of friends or family or co-workers has value because it provides such a rich source of knowledge for how other people do things. We may become fascinated with the corner of a mouth, the droop of an eye, the move of a hand, the sound of a voice, the manner of speaking or the subtlety of response.

Keith

Keith Williams is developing new skills as he learns how to be a working engineer instead of a star graduate student. "I've been preoccupied with how to dress, how to handle the first few minutes of an interview and how to present myself in a work situation. I'm having to sort through my values, decide which are mine, which were taught me in school and which are my parents. The big question is, "What does that leave me with?"

Brenda

Brenda H., at age 42, had three forces contributing to her need to carry out Stage Five tasks. Her inner clock signaled a biological return at the same time she decided to make a career change that required learning new skills. Added to that was her daughter turning nine. "There's a lot of arguing going on around our house," she confided. "At first I was real stubborn. I wanted to push everybody away, as if I couldn't have my own values and still be close. I had to learn how to hassle all over again. In the beginning I put people down and thought somebody had to lose. Now I'm learning about how to argue with caring in it, where both people can win. We have very few exchanges that are just plain, 'will you . . . yes, no.' Instead, I have my jaw out, being at odds and wanting other people to say out loud whether they agree or disagree. It's important that they're willing to argue about something.

"I need to check out my why's against theirs, such as, 'Why wouldn't this be better?' 'Why don't you like something?' 'What's fair?'

'What are the rules?' or 'Why are those the rules?' Life is more fun when I get my values straightened out. I'm more flexible. I'm more interested in what's going on. At the same time I have a take-charge attitude. I get things going, snap, snap, snap. It's not that I'm bossy, just more directive and efficient. Finding new ways to let my creative energies out is a real challenge."

In Stage Five our concerns include, "How do I structure my day, week, year or life?" "What's important?" "Are the same things important to you that are important to me?" or "Why do you choose that way to live?"

To create new methods, we learn by *doing*, planting a garden, making bread, chopping wood or making a sale. We want to know how other people do it, but also how to argue with the why they've chosen. We need others' models as a basis for putting together our own.

This is the time we deal with the authorities of our life (bosses, ministers, lawyers, judges, mothers, guides and experts). We pursue such arguments as, "I'm sure the rules are not as you're describing," "In fact, I read about that the other day," "And besides, my friend told me," "And furthermore, when I was little," "Besides, my mother always . . . ." We search out new social roles; for example, we say, "When I grow up I want to be . . .," "I'm tired of staying home with the kids — I think I'll get a job," "This work's too taxing and besides, I miss the kids," "I think I'll find an easier line of work," "I know I'm not ready to be a father," or "I'm ready to be a student."

Regardless of how old we are, each time we experience such symptoms of Stage Five, we need to do the following developmental tasks in order to develop our *Power of Being Skillful:*

1. To experiment with different ways of doing things
2. To develop physical, intellectual, emotional and social skills
3. To argue, hassle and disagree
4. To exclude others' methods until we make our own
5. To learn new morals, manners or values
6. To make mistakes in order to find out what works
   (Techniques are at the end of this chapter.)

Setting The Stage For The Power Of Being

During the later years of childhood we concentrate on developing the skills we think are necessary to survive in the world independently. We learn how to tie shoelaces, to cross the street, to read and write and even to moralize. We want to learn how to be effective and to say with confidence, "I can do it." We develop our own code of values based on our unique experiences creating structures or organized models that define and describe the world; e.g., "Think," "Work hard," "Take your time," "Don't get smart," or "Use your smarts." These elements we can add to our own experiences. Using others' structures as a basis for argument, we create, test and improve our own skills in the world.

To create our own skills we use a process called *excluding*. This involves both inviting structures from others and defending against them at the same time. Then we argue or hassle as a way of taking parts of others' skills or values and making them our own. When translated into eight-year-old language, *excluding* means children this age are name callers. Someone who doesn't answer a question is labeled stupid. A little pimple earns the label of leper. The slightest limp becomes the subject of controversy. Although this may seem insensitive, it serves an important developmental function. Excluding behavior is essential for building structure.

The methods and morals we create here provide the final ingredient in the recipe for a complete personality. This personal, internalized technology for living protects us automatically. If we're about to run in the street, this part automatically yells, "Stop!" without the lengthy process that thinking requires. We each invent these life-supporting structures through doing or interacting to have our own experiences.

The type of structures we create are so important because once established, they preselect information. In addition, the first methods we develop are the template on which we build the skills of living throughout life. We are literally *learning how to learn how.*

The kind of skills we develop and the ease with which we develop them are affected and even limited by our experiences and decisions in previous stages. For example, Stage Two conclusions (about doing things and deciding whether or not it is even safe to do things) that we made when we were crawling, support or limit what we *do* in Stage Five to build skills.

Identity conclusions in Stage Four also play a determining role. Our decision about which gender we are serves as a basis for whether we develop male or female models, or both, in Stage Five.

Opposite sex structures are often excluded on that basis alone as each child creates structures consistent with our identity. In Stage Four, the question was, "Am I a boy or girl?" In Stage Five we answer, "*How* to be a boy or girl."

To accomplish this we may learn skills that are consistent with genital equipment rather than those consistent with needs. Boys may learn bread-winning while girls learn bread-baking. We may learn sex-appropriate appearances, behavior and values rather than structures that meet needs. Boys may learn to play with guns, to be rugged and to touch whereas girls may learn to play quietly, to look pretty and to sit still. Boys may be groomed to become the creators and controllers, and girls to become the sustainers and the controlled. He may learn to always argue but she, not to do so. Boys may learn to go after what they want, whereas girls may learn to look pretty and wait for it to come into their vicinity. Thus, boys may learn to be aggressive and girls learn to be passive. Both may learn what the male defines as "normal", so that aggression, a master-class trait, is normal (okay), and passivity, a subject group trait, is abnormal (not-okay).

As children in Stage Five, our interest in sex revolves around the mechanics of *how* to do it, because we're not yet ready to learn other aspects of being sexual. We're interested in exploring each others' bodies, particularly those of the same sex, as part of the process of learning how to be a boy or girl.

We develop the *Power of Being Skillful* in our family and in our culture as we learn what roles and behavior are considered appropriate to our sex and social position. These roles become primary ways of relating to other people and groups. Familiar statements relating to these roles include, "The Hatfields are better than the McCoys" or "We may be poor folks, but we're honest" or "What is male is normal and what is female is abnormal; what is white is normal and what is black, red or yellow is inferior." Ageism, sexism, racism — all may be passed from generation to generation through the "how to's" created during this stage.

Cycle Sabotage In Stage Five

When we "hurry" through Stage Five, we're likely to become skillful in acting competent even though feeling scared and hiding it.

We may develop patterns of relating to others by having opinions, by arguing and by discussing morals, but not by being close, intimate and open. The way we define reality for ourselves is designed to protect us by keeping people at a distance. We say, "Stay away from dependency needs," "Learn how to push other people away," "Wait until nothing worse can happen," "Don't think about fear" or "Use your values to reject others."

When we "stay little" we may attempt to avoid Stage Five entirely by continuing to borrow others' values and morals instead of creating our own. We may learn how to act little and incompetent, how to hide thinking and how to keep others close as ways of staying safe. We may develop patterns of relating to others by pointing out our relative lack of skill compared to them or how easily we are overwhelmed and have difficulty coping. The way we define reality is designed to keep others close, such as "Stay little," "Be dependent," "Get others motivated and do it for you," "Sacrifice your own position," "Don't structure," and "Don't think about anger."

Both patterns lead to suffering when doing things[28] by preventing us from using our own methods on our own behalf. These deviations restrict our skillfulness by excluding the developmental tasks we need to carry out to create and expand our repertoire of skills. The more we use these deviations, the more we create frustration.

During this stage we may also take on cultural values that support our failing to develop certain skills. We may learn to substitute material things or gadgets for the people contact we need; or we may compete with friends instead of cooperating for the goodies life has to offer. We may limit what we do to goal directed behavior, giving up the richness of exploratory activity. We may (1) learn to conform to authority instead of developing independence or (2) learn to use skills consistent with our genital equipment instead of those consistent with our needs. Especially, we may base our relationships on producing something instead of developing our mutual potential for power.

We may act rigid and unyielding if we accepted someone else's way of doing things without making it our own. In addition, we may feel angry when being active instead of the joy that comes from doing something well.

We may have decided that learning skills has negative consequences and is to be avoided because we believe that we'll be required to do it all the time. For example, "There, now you know how to do the dishes, you can do them from now on."

When we take on methods and skills in conflict with our needs, the effect is like that of taking on an internal, bossy and judgmental attitude. This aspect defines us as lacking something, such as "You're a failure and you'll stay a failure, but try to make it anyway" or "Be a victim, work hard and drink a lot."

Stage Five Games [29, 30]

1. **Courtroom** is played in competition for "who gets to be right" and therefore who gets the goodies (attention, money) by people whose childhood experiences in developing skills left them believing they were always wrong and therefore had to suffer or feel bad. By not excluding others' structures, they turned this problem-solving mechanism in on themselves, excluding their own needs and feelings.

2. **Ain't It Awful** is played by people who never got beyond excluding. This temporary developmental device becomes the cornerstone of their skills in relating. Their own prohibition about doing things their own way motivates them to cluck disapprovingly at others' methods instead of developing better alternatives.

3. **Blemish** is played to ward off depression while keeping others at a distance. The player protects against an internal feeling of being victimized by judging others.

4. **P.T.A.** is played to ward off guilt. Instead of doing something about problems, the players merely talk about them, judging others' effort negatively.

5. **Now I've Got You, You Son-of-a-Bitch** is played by people who use their skills to pin responsibility for failure on to others, waiting until others make a mistake and then trapping them in it.

Body Language Of Being Skillful

Body problems from this stage of development often manifest in our physical *structure,* such as spinal misalignments, lordosis, kyphosis and scoliosis; coordination problems; difficulty with motor skills; lack of development or hyperdevelopment of skeletal muscles, particularly in the upper chest; and muscular binding in the upper chest and back, especially where the diaphragm inserts on the last thoracic and first lumbar vertebrae.

Other Stage Five physical problems are related to specific values. For example, back pain may occur from the value that "to be a man is to do backbreaking labor"; perspiration may be inhibiting because "ladies don't sweat"; or excess fatty tissue may be carried from burdensome values such as "take care of everybody else first".

Structures that subdue and override the person they were supposedly invented to support can inhibit our sexuality by blocking, repressing or otherwise controlling body energy.

You may have power potential to develop in Stage Five: (1) if you act as if someone said, "Don't think, just do it," "Don't structure," "Don't exclude," "Don't argue," and "Don't make mistakes," or (2) if "Don't know how," "Can't do it (my way, your way)," and "(I'm, you're, it's) not okay . . . dumb, lazy, stupid," are recurrent themes for you.

Reclaiming The Power Of Being Skillful

The following studies demonstrate how to reclaim our *Power of Being Skillful.*

Karen

Karen Gehrman may have repeated Stage Five several times, but she'd show little evidence of it. She didn't argue; instead she adapted. She was expected to quit her job teaching when she married, and she did. She was expected to stay home and raise the children, and she did. She was expected to be a diligent member of the Junior League, and she was. "I did the housework, too, but I resented it," she said.

When her older son began the hassling he needed to do in Stage Five, the whole family was thrown into conflict. "He was trying to become his own person, strong and independent and so was I. We clashed continuously. I felt as if I was being held down, as if my mother was controlling me and as if my husband was controlling me. I decided to do something about being a pleaser, an adapter, and one not to make waves. I wanted to change my life."

At the same time Ken (her husband) had attained his goal in life by becoming the head of a department at a bank. Karen said, "He started thinking, 'This is what I've worked for all my life, big deal!' We spent a year talking and sorting out what we really wanted to do and what our parents wanted us to. We got some professional help along the way, too. We both found out it was okay to disagree, make waves and talk about things. Ken decided to become more involved with the family and children. I loved nature and the country and we decided to buy a cabin in the mountains. We improved our relationship considerably that way."

A few years later, however, at 42 years of age, Karen's internal clock pointed to a time to recycle Stage Five at the same time her second child was growing through Stage Five for the first time, bringing up issues from her own childhood.

"I realized I was never allowed to argue and hassle. It was always, 'This is the way things are'. I felt very angry about it. I had to find a way to get rid of that anger somewhere else, and maybe I did it by being sick. I believed that you really do have to suffer to get attention. I knew if I was sick, I'd get the love I needed. I had a lot of allergies. I think a lot of them were dreamed up. I was buying the love I needed. I was an only child until I was sick, oops, I mean *six*, and then my brother was born.

"My husband's family literally never got sick, and so my childhood game didn't work in adulthood. From the time I got married I started having a dream of a very powerful figure standing over me and I was paralyzed. I remember screaming and trying to wake up. I couldn't do anything because this powerful figure kept pushing me down. I think that represented the power I was allowing my mother and father and husband to have over me."

Karen's internal clock, her second son being in Stage Five and her old ways of doing things that no longer worked were three powerful forces which converged and impelled her to dive deeper into the root of her difficulties. Curious about her own childhood, Karen asked her mother what she remembered. "She confirmed my feeling that I missed a whole lot between six and 12. My mother said that she was so busy with my brother she didn't remember what I was like until I was 12 or 13. So I started going back, thinking about those ages. I'd taken an assertiveness class to learn to make waves and I'd read books on constructive arguing, but still something was missing. I knew I needed something more. Meanwhile, my blood pressure had been creeping up over the years. The doctors had started me on a diuretic pill, and then a couple of other pills. None of them had any effect."

At first Karen thought the way to get free of her powerful mother was to reject her. "I thought, 'I don't need you. I don't need that stuff. I'm not going to listen to you anymore.' Then, as time went on, I realized I did need her to tell me she loved me and to tell me she cared. She didn't have to feel for me, to think for me or to control me. I could handle that. I needed to know she loved me for *me*, not for what I did. I was tired of doing things in order to get love."

At a weekend problem-solving group, Karen was one of the first to say that she wanted to work. Someone else had mentioned needing to be an infant again, and Karen became furious. "I thought, 'Some baby is going to dethrone me again.' I had never gone back to a former age before. I knew I needed to be six, but I didn't know how. I thought it was a magical process, but there I was, being six and angry. When I was little and angry with my mother, I used to go into my closet and throw all the shoes out. This time I pounded on a pillow and wadded up paper and threw it, each time telling her (as if her mother were there) that I was angry. Then I realized I was afraid she was going to go away, and afraid that if I didn't do what people who loved me wanted me to do, they'd get angry and go away. She always threatened that if things weren't the way she wanted them, she would leave. I started saying, 'I need you to love me.' I decided to stop being a nice little girl and start being *me* and saying what I wanted."

The rest of the weekend Karen reclaimed and developed her *Power of Being Skillful*. For example, she argued about how others were doing things and found out nobody left her. She also began developing new skills for getting attention other than being sick. When she didn't like something in a play group, instead of getting sick she planned a birthday party and invited all her friends. Later in the evening, with some other grown-up "kids" her age, she played cards and argued about the rules. Then she left saying, "I'll be right back," but didn't come back for a long time. "They all sat and waited! I thought, 'those dummies, they waited when they could have played without me!' But they didn't leave or get angry, either one."

Later Karen reported while she was doing this work of a six-year-old, "I heard my stomach sigh! Before that, if I'd heard somebody start to argue, my stomach would tighten and hurt, but not since that weekend. And later, the doctor was surprised to tell me my blood pressure had dropped! That's not to say everything's been perfect since. For one thing, Ken and I really locked horns for a little while after that. I kept telling him I really resented it when he thought for me or told me how to feel. For another, I had an opportunity to teach a class on the same night my son needed me to take him somewhere. A year ago I'd have said, 'It's my role as a mother to be there for my children.' But I got the family together and told them how important it was for me to teach, and we worked out an arrangement so that I could do it. And the big one is, I am not afraid of my anger!"

People who are finishing Stage Five tasks often find they become closer to people of the same sex. They may also create a new cultural role for themselves. Some go back to school, some discover a creative gift in art or music. Karen is considering going back to school to get her master's degree. Meanwhile she is enjoying a classic form of women's art. She is making quilts for the beds at their cabin.

For those who may have missed something in this stage she advises, "Think about those years, what it was really like and how you'd like it to be. Then go to the park and watch healthy children that age. See what they're doing . . . arguing, hassling, disagreeing or whatever. You can even work with them to find out how they operate. And read books like *Tom Sawyer* to get a feeling for what you need to do."

George and Martha

George, age 45, and Martha, age 42, had developed a pattern in their marriage. They held delightful dinner parties, which were followed by demoralizing quarrels. Martha would be furious. "You just sit there with that calm expression on your face. Why don't you say anything? I never know what's going on!" George responded, "You're always so unreasonable, jumping up and down like that, blaming it on me. You must be upset. Maybe you're getting your period."

They related together as though they had only one complete personality between the two of them, attached to each other by an umbilical cord of complementary functions. George could nurture, criticize, protect and think for Martha, while she could express needs, wants, desires, fears and hurts for George.

Outside their relationship George was a competent person in a business world of production deadlines. He knew how to make a sale, close a deal and deliver the goods. Yet he was also secretive, emotionally distant and argumentative, "To hell with how you feel about it, just get the job done!" he'd tell Martha when she said she was starved for affection. "I've got to take care of business, think about what should happen tomorrow." Martha, meanwhile, knew how to play the child. Instead of defining reality for herself, she adapted to the morals and methods of others, especially to what George expected of her. In his absence, she copied from others, especially imitating women in fashion magazines.

The first time George had an opportunity to develop his *Power of Being Skillful* in childhood, his father was absent, sometimes in mind and often in body. George did little editing of values, but instead took them directly from the movies or radio. Without the reality-check that arguing would have provided, George felt insecure and ill-prepared for life outside his family. Upon graduation from high school, he joined the military. Later he became compulsive about earning money. At 45, well-off financially, he reviewed this situation angrily. In a depressed state he questioned, "Where will I end up, dead in a foxhole or dead in a coronary unit? I'm not living my life my way and I'm churning inside."

In Martha's girlhood the pattern was similar. Her mother was around but unavailable for arguing or pushing. Martha got attention from her father, who was pleased by her staying his little girl, expressing feelings and being soft and feminine. Martha saw no other acceptable ways to be a girl. The women in her small town all deferred to and took care of men, except those labeled "loose" or "old maids".

In the absence of effective parenting in childhood, both George and Martha had latched onto cultural stereotypes in order to get by. They continued this pattern in adulthood, marrying and assuming all the manners and mores of "success". They had a lot of money, owned a boat, took expensive vacations, wore stylish clothes, lived in a big house and entertained lavishly. Meanwhile a gnawing empty lack of purpose filled their lives and slowly ate away at the pretenses. They decided to get to the root of it and find a better way.

As a part of that process they both became members of a group where seeing others finishing developmental tasks triggered responses in both of them. As part of reclaiming his *Power of Being Skillful,* George arranged a camping trip with the group leader. He functioned at the level of an eight-year-old while learning about fishing, camping and carrying out tasks. He even dared to cross his new, temporary father, to invite anger, to argue and to experiment with different ways of doing things without losing affection.

Martha did much of her work of an eight-year-old arguing with the group members, "Why did you confront him then?" or "Why not earlier?" or "Don't you think she needs a homework assignment?" or "Do you ever wear lipstick?" or "I think you should wear your hair short" or "Do you like my new outfit?" It was as if she held a magnifying glass, surveying the women. Soon she took over the job of buying snacks for the meeting and hassling about what kind of food to buy. She drew anger from one of the men by refusing to purchase his favorite candy. "They're not good for you; they rot your teeth!" she insisted, holding her position. Then, to test her new ability to do things her own way and have her own skills, Martha took a big step and left on a vacation alone.

When she returned she was eager to develop new ways of relating to George while still maintaining her own values and abilities. She joined a drama company and soon her interest developed into a career as an actress. To develop an atmosphere of loving strength together, they learned skills to maintain their relationship, with praise, approval, gift-giving, wrestling, massage and negotiating. They frequently disagreed on what's important or how to handle situations. For George, having two people live two lives instead of one is quite a difference; it supports his having his own feelings and therefore his own direction in life. For Martha, the difference is being able to have her own values and skills and to feel secure in knowing she can earn her own living. She is happy to live with George out of choice instead of necessity.

Stage Six: The Power Of Regeneration

The omnipresent process of sex, as it is woven into the whole texture of a man's or woman's body, is the pattern of all the process of our life.

Havelock Ellis

Summary

This stage has particular significance for those who are:

- 13 through 18 years
- after establishing new skills
- when preparing to complete anything, leave a relationship, job, home, social group, organization, locality

- when making changes in our sexuality
- at ages which are multiples of 13, 14, 15, 16, 17 and 18

Affirmations

It's okay for you to be sexual, to have a place among grown-ups and to succeed.
You can be a sexual person and still have needs.
It's okay to be responsible for your own needs, feelings and
   behavior.
It's okay to be on your own.
You're welcome to come home again.
My love goes with you.

Normal Symptoms

Symptoms can include succumbing to episodes of dependency with urges to explore and be separate; being preoccupied with sex and with people as sexual beings; having discomfort or pain and tingling in sexual organs; experiencing acne or other skin eruptions and turbulent bodily changes, especially rapid fluctuations in hormone and energy levels; needing to unify our personality; creating our own independent support system and developing social relationships as a sexual person.

Deviations

Hurry Up. This means using sexual behavior to avoid and control dependency needs.
Stay Little. This means using nurturing behavior to avoid and control sexual urges.

Developing Power Of Regeneration

Stage Six is the bridge from childhood to adulthood, a transition from old to new, from the end of the last cycle to the beginning of the next one, the phase in which the seed is made for the new beginning.

Karen

Karen Malgren is now in her early 50s and her children are all grown-up. She lives in the southwest United States where she manages a university placement office. "I feel like yelling 'help' most of the time," she said. "I'm about as confident as a teenager on her first date. And I'm mad, too. I don't want to mess this up! It's about this man I've gone out with several times. I saw him on the tennis courts yesterday with another woman. He's so tender, gentle, complimentary when we're together so that I feel I can do no wrong. Then I see him with this woman . . . and she went to his apartment, too. I'm tired of being with him one night and then seeing him with somebody else the next! Part of me wants to break off our relationship or pretend we don't even have one! I've got pains in my shoulders that just won't quit. I know that will lead to headaches if I don't do something about what I'm feeling!"

Ralph

Ralph MacKenzie had been thinking about how old he's getting. After he celebrated his 32nd birthday, he said, "I realize my sexual life and my physical body are not exhausted and used up. Life is not over! I have vitality and strength and have matured. That awakening whets my sexual appetite. At the same time I have the desire to bring my body into balance, to rebuild muscle and sinew in order to feel as alive as I can. This time I feel my life is no longer infinite. When I was an adolescent (the first time) I thought my body could take anything and I'd live forever. Now I have a desire to take care of my body, to nourish it with a regular routine as opposed to abusing it as I did when I was 16 and went for days and nights without sleep. I'm realizing my body is a vehicle for the kind of life I want to live. I want to exercise some discretion about drinking, smoking and carousing, the habits that use up my energy. That way I'll still be able to live a youthful life even though I'm getting older.

"I want to live my sexual fantasies and to experiment now because I know it won't go on forever. I still have that virility and a strong desire to use it while I have it.

"I'm putting together what's happened in my life up to this point. When I was 16 I broke with the traditional philosophies that bound me . . . I willfully pushed aside the morality of my family and society. Now, at 32 I have that renewed urge to push again, but in a creative way that doesn't just rebel, but builds. I want to go beyond what's been done and leave my mark. At 16 I had a dream; at 32 I want to make it real."

Stage Six symbolizes regeneration in all its aspects. Through the tasks we carry out here we undergo a complete moral reform, bringing into existence again the previous stages of our lives. The cycle gives us the possibility of regenerating ourselves as we renew, restore and grow new levels of being from old ones. At the same time we develop the ability to give birth to others.

The signs of entering Stage Six are both subtle and overt. There is often dreaminess, a preoccupation with things internal, unseen, unknown or yet to be. There is fascination with sex, sex, sex! Our previous concern with being competent and skillful seems somehow not applicable, not even relevant in this unshaped territory. We simply need to learn to be here and to exist in this dream.

As grown-ups repeating this stage we may still feel lost, adrift in an uncharted land and even sexually naive and virginal. We may want to stop having sex temporarily, to change partners or to change the patterns in a relationship. Our new, sexual desires and the developmental tasks from the previous five stages require integration. We will come out of this process relating to the world in a new and grown-up way, having moved beyond relationships that once were the mainstay for our support.

Themes from previous stages recur in short episodes as we briefly revisit them in order to unify our various functions into one personality. It is a natural opportunity to reclaim power by resolving earlier problems.

Regardless of our age, each time we revisit Stage Six we need to do the following developmental tasks to develop the *Power of Regeneration:*

1. To integrate sexuality with needs from other stages
2. To grow beyond our parenting (mentoring or other supportive) relationships
3. To develop our own personal philosophy

4. To deal with being sexual changes and develop as a sexually mature person
5. To revisit each earlier stage
6. To find and develop a place among grown-ups

(Exercises for meeting these needs are listed in Part III, Chapter 8.)

Setting The Stage For The Power Of Regeneration

Starting with this stage we are no longer developing new parts of our personality because we already have them. Instead, we have a second opportunity to develop:

The Power of Being. At 13 we may experience a powerful resurgence of the need to be taken care of, to stop doing and be close and intimate, to bond and connect. It is a step into maturity and back into dependency all in one.

The onset of dependency needs along with sexual changes affects all relationships. Parents, brothers and sisters may become cautious of closeness because they're uncertain about whether incest is a feeling or an action. Nonetheless, physical contact is basic to healthy development in Stage Six. During this time we have a short, almost nonexistent attention span. We're unmotivated to think, preferring instead to feel, to daydream, to stare off into space or into the mirror to check our appearance.

The Power of Doing. A short revisit to our exploratory stage is next. We become interested in sensory satisfaction rather than goals. Themes resurface about doing, especially as it relates to getting taken care of. Carrying out activities for no reason other than to do something may seem illogical to those in older stages of the cycle, but it is not. We are feeding our senses, improving our body coordination and building a bridge out of dependency as we explore.

The Power of Thinking. During this time, at about age 14, we return to negativity, wanting to say no and to exert our independence. We may deal with anger or overstep our bounds just to see what happens. We may be sloppy one moment and fussy the next. (That strawberry jam is so gooey on the rug!) We may create social anguish for ourselves due to trouble remembering things. (What was his name, anyway?) Even so, we are discovering a knack for learning new facts and developing new capacities to think.

The Power of Identity. Around age 15 we experience a short, intense visit to Stage Four, a time of developing who we are. We may return, temporarily, to old identity issues. During this time we have easy access to the decision we made at age four. In addition, we may find ourselves needing to answer all over again, "Who am I?" or "What is my life about?" We want to test power, find differences between people and set up disagreements between them. We return to an active interest in genital equipment, especially the *differences* between boys and girls; this time we add the sexual appetite of adolescence. We may test our power to do "magic" and may scare, hurt or enrage ourselves or others, all in rapid succession.

Nightmares, intense bouts of fantasy and the urge to tell "lies" (stories) or take other people's belongings just to see what happens may become temporary, if not everyday occurrences.

The Power of Being Skillful. Around age 16, we begin actively stepping beyond the parameters of our parents', teachers' or mentors' values as we break out of those relationships to establish ourselves as grown-ups. As a preacher's kid we may do something hideously unholy; as the child of a teacher we may grow enamored of an uneducated lifestyle. At this point we review the hopes, disappointments and fond memories of the past at the same time that we create dreams and plans for the future.

The design of the cycle dictates what our tasks are in Stage Six, but culture influences how they will be carried out. For example, girls may be given cultural responsibility for regulating and controlling sexual contact. They may be defined as only wanting sex in order to become pregnant but otherwise not having a sexual urge. Girls may feel they are encouraged to resist their sexuality and so may develop an "I won't" attitude about sex, becoming more and more resistive to the approach of a possible partner. Girls, fearing pregnancy and social ostracism, may learn to be the "no sayer".

Injunctions girls may receive include:

Be appreciative but challenging (don't give in too easily).
Be vulnerable but protect yourself.
Be smart enough to get a man but interested in only one.
Be desired by all but interested in only one.

Be sophisticated but naive.
Be sexy but stay a virgin.

Boys may be given a free reign from responsibility around sexual contact or prevention of pregnancy. They may be encouraged to see their sexual urges as so strong (grandiose) as to be difficult for them to control. Boys may learn to wheedle, appease and catch girls in a moment of weakness.

Messages boys receive may include:

Take care of girls as the way to deal with sexuality.
If you're going to mess around, don't get her pregnant.
Play around but don't get caught (trapped).
Be strong, be cool (don't show feelings, except sexual ones).
It's okay to have sex, but don't get involved.

Cultural scripting may reach such adaptations as boys learning to look big and masterful whereas girls lean to look small. Adaptation to "ideal" size differences among the sexes can lead to all sorts of postural difficulties as well as feelings of inadequacy.

Cycle Sabotage In Stage Six

Difficulties from a previous stage may recur in a more sophisticated, often sexual form in Stage Six. "I can't get enough (nurturing)" from Stage One may become "I can't get enough (sex)" in Stage Six. "I can't separate from you" in Stage Three may become ". . . and therefore I can't become a sexual person." Two patterns are common. One is to seek sexual contact instead of meeting the need for nurturing; the other is to take care of others or get them to take care of us instead of responding to sexual urges.

When we leave developmental tasks unfinished in adolescence, they may reappear during adulthood as problems defining reality, lacking a personal philosophy of life, lacking a support system outside the family or having difficulty being sexual. We just don't get on with our life. We may be sexually active but set things up to yield bad feelings instead of satisfaction because we didn't take the time to learn how to be a sexually mature person.

Being successful in the world is linked to Stage Six developmental tasks. Everyone fails many times in learning to succeed, but people with Stage Six problems don't make necessary adjustments and continue toward their goal, pointing to unfinished business in growing beyond their parents.[31]

We may interpret loss of contact to mean that becoming sexual is dangerous to our survival needs. We may inhibit our sexual development as a result, or decide to use sex as a substitute for getting taken care of. We may also develop skin eruptions when we fail to meet needs for the physically affectionate, nonsexual touch, which can often reduce or eliminate skin problems.

Bodily symptoms and games from each previous stage are likely to be repeated in more exaggerated form. In addition, these physical symptoms are common: having pain in the long muscles, especially the legs; experiencing discomfort in sex organs or glands; having diminished development of secondary sex characteristics; lacking sexual appetite; having skin eruptions; being impotent; having premature ejaculation and inorgasmic responses.

If you act as if someone said, "Don't make it," "Don't grow up," "Don't succeed," or "Don't be sexual," you may have untapped power potential to develop in Stage Six.

Reclaiming The Power Of Regeneration

Tania's and Carrie's life experiences are illustrations of Stage Six, *Reclaiming the Power of Regeneration.*

Tania

Tania Kruger's first adolescence left a few things to be desired. For one thing, she entered it ill-prepared because she was not allowed to play as a child. "Fun was simply not okay; it was idleness," she said. "Then it was very important to always be clean and not messy, because it's important what other people think and they don't like messy little girls," she continued.

She first learned about babies and, by inference, about sex, not from her family, but when a nurse in a hospital where Tania stayed overnight left the door to the delivery room open. A woman delivered an infant by natural childbirth. "It was gorgeous," she said. "I was so impressed!" Afterward the nurse talked to her, explaining the names of body parts and so forth. It was a kind, inspiring initiation even if it wasn't by her parents.

The next awakening came at 15 at a piano recital. The fellow behind her said that he thought she ought to go to the bathroom. She excused herself and found a great big red blob on the back of her beautiful new light blue suit.

When she was 16, still ill-informed on the facts of life, her parents told her in no uncertain terms that if she ever came home pregnant she'd have no home to come to. She became petrified, thinking, "If I get close to a guy I'm going to get pregnant. That's when I started smoking," she said. "For me smoking and sexuality have a big link."

She attended a year of business school after high school graduation, then got a job and at 19 got married. "I was still just as ignorant as I was when I was a teenager. The marriage scene was the beginning of my sexuality. I'd never even masturbated except when I was real little. I can still see myself walking away as we were going on our honeymoon. My dad said, 'For God sake, kid, be good to him,' which I now interpret as, 'Don't ever say no.' Mother said, 'Remember, honey, it's going to hurt.' And she was right." It was two weeks before they were able to consummate the marriage, so tense was the bride.

"I pulled right into a shell," she said. "There was never any foreplay and then it was always, 'Did you come?' I learned to lie very quickly because if I didn't, he felt inadequate and then he'd be a bastard to live with. For 18 years I thought I must be frigid." And she suffered from stomach pains daily, waking up at night to drink cream to quell the pain.

When their children reached adolescence Tania began to lose weight. "If I were to answer then how big I felt my space was, I'd say about 97 pounds. Here I was with my shoulders up around my ear lobes, my arms very tightly held into my body indicating how I felt inside. I was the wife of a successful businessman, but all of us wives lived a facade of masks, makeup, fake eyelashes and wigs. I volunteered for everything. That tied in with not feeling important because only important people earn money; the unimportant ones volunteer." Her life, she realized, closely followed the pattern of her parents who had lived together with almost no sex life until her father

died of a cerebral hemorrhage at 49. A week before his death he told
Tania that he wanted a divorce and didn't have the guts to do it.

"I realized I could stay with the marriage and probably die at 49 like
my dad did or do something about it." Then she met a man who was
turned on to her sexually and she reciprocated. Still, the decision was
difficult; divorce would mean giving up security, a known relationship
and prestige. Finally she decided to do it, telling the corporate wives
who'd been encouraging her to divorce for the last ten years. "They all
vanished; it must have been too risky for them to accept," she said.

"When I decided to leave, my own trust level raised significantly.
I decided to take the risk, and admitted it was okay to make a
mistake. If I needed to deal with sexuality that was okay too."

Gradually she set up an outside support system by getting involved
in a growth movement organization. "I needed the kind of people
who are allowers," she said. "People who would allow me to be and
do my own thing even though it might not be what they would do.

She listed her fears in order of priority in one column and in the
next defined actual reality. The same day she began masturbating for
the first time in her life. Slowly and deeply she became aware of how
much of her life's energies were going into taking care of others,
particularly men instead of herself. "I needed to receive support from
other people, and to know they were glad I was learning to take care
of myself. That was especially important from women and I got that
from three women friends. I needed it from men, too, saying things
like, 'I really think you did the right thing. Gee, you look great. It's
nice to see you taking care of yourself.' I needed to get protection
from people who were like a nurturing mother and father who'd
answer my questions and share."

This time she decided to really learn how to be sexual, not just to
do it. At one point she asked her lover, "What you're doing feels so
strange, so wonderful. Why are you doing this?"

And he said, "I just want to feel all of you. I want to know how all
of you feels."

She further related, "I realized, of course, that is what many people
forget in wanting to be sexual — that physical stroking is the biggest
thing. Just relaxing, getting to know each other's bodies and enjoying
the pleasure whether it leads to orgasms or not. In the few years since
the beginning of our relationship I learned to enjoy my own body
and to feel my body is okay and interesting enough. In that time I've

increased my bra three or four sizes. I think a good deal of it was simple acceptance, enjoying our sexual relationship. I started unwinding, muscle by muscle, little by little."

Part of her change, too, was realizing how much she needed to be taken care of rather than taking care of other people. In a relationship with a therapist who knew how to be a good mother, Tania went back to deal with some basic trust issues as an infant. "Just thinking about how safe and warm and comfortable that was makes it hard to sit up," she laughed. "That was my first experience being held and taking a bottle, and it was really neat and extremely sensual. I was amazed and excited. That was the beginning of unfolding the flower. The changes I'd made on the surface level hadn't been enough. Being taken care of was an essential part of my integration process, moving the new knowledge from my head to my belly."

Tania changed her life in many ways by finishing the developmental tasks she'd left behind in adolescence and in infancy. First she doesn't have pains in her stomach anymore. Second, she trusts herself. "I know that when the time is right I will do what I need to do. I didn't know that before. I feel confident, too, realizing, 'Oh, my God, I really can do something.' I can make the decision to take risks. And I have my own philosophy . . . especially that being a sexual person is okay and having sex is okay." She's made changes in her work, too. She'd started out as a part-time accountant's assistant. Now she's getting ready to establish a practice of her own and to officially hang out her shingle.

To others who need to do similar work she advises, "Do it. It's fun. It's rewarding and you're worth it. You're here for a reason and you're not going to find out why you're here until you get to know all of who you are, including you as a sexual person. Do it without negative reinforcement as much as possible. Don't pretend your partner's free if that's not true, or that you're free if you're not. That's something to be dealt with, not discounted. Go ahead and open up. If you shut off you're going to be floundering around wondering which way to go. Internal direction will guide you."

Carrie

Carrie S. was raised the same way as many people of German parentage are, with a lot of inflexible rules, which she described as "either black or white, with no grey in between". Her mother was long-suffering but intelligent. She taught her daughter to think, but not about what she needed. Her father loved his daughter very much. Unfortunately he didn't know how to relate to people very well. Though very physically attractive, he seemed awkward and ambivalent at the attention this brought. Both parents immobilized themselves. Carrie imitated them.

At the end of the fourth grade, at age 10, Carrie's mother took her daughter for a walk in the woods and talked about the physiology of sex. "I really froze," Carrie shivered in recollection. "She had such a strange energy. I stopped thinking. I kept saying to myself, 'When is she going to stop?' I knew things would just get worse if I said, 'Please stop.' She described all the male and female anatomy but if you'd asked me who did what, I couldn't have told you. It wasn't until I was 20 that I figured out a penis goes into a vagina." Later that night her mother ended the lecture with a parting shot as she tucked her daughter into bed. "If any man should ever get you in a car and take you away and pull down your panties, and, and, . . . oh, I just don't know what I'd do." And she turned off the light and left the room. Carrie was incredibly confused and scared. All that night she kept seeing spiders in her bed.

Outgoing Carrie gradually withdrew. She refused phone calls from boys who'd been her friends. As she became a teenager she studied more and socialized less. At age 15, after her mother insisted she go swimming, she locked herself in the bathroom of a motel where she was staying with her parents rather than go down to the pool in a bathing suit. Her mother reacted to this strange behavior by crawling into her husband's lap and crying like a baby while he looked uncomfortable but did nothing.

Later the same year Carrie told her mother that she wanted to see a psychiatrist because she had a big problem and she needed help. Her mother became hysterical, saying "My children are not mental cases and they don't need to see a psychiatrist." Carrie went to see a Catholic priest but he didn't know what to do either. So she decided not to do anything about it for a while.

She finessed her way out of the high school prom by judging it too childish. "I wanted so much to dance," she said. "But I couldn't do it. It was too sexual and I felt unprotected. Once I remember sobbing on Daddy's shoulder, saying 'Daddy, I'm just scared of men. I don't know what to do.' And he said, 'I know. I don't know what to do either.' " By the time she was 16 there were only two males she would talk to, her father and her nephew seven years younger. Like a child attempting to protect herself magically she developed a range of obsessions, and although she loved the outdoors she stayed away from it. "It was too threatening because you have to move and you have to have a body outdoors." She took her mother's nagging her to date with silence. She simply had no interest, she told her.

In college and away from home she began to thaw out slowly, cautiously, having two dates the first year. The second year she became platonic friends with some men in her classes and began to see that men were human. Then she became a counselor at a coed summer camp. "I decided then it's about time I found out what sex is about. So when I got home from camp I moved out of the house and called one of the men from camp. I thought he was pretty decent and wouldn't do me dirty so I said, 'I'll go to bed with you.' Within a split second I decided I was in love with him. (It wouldn't have been okay for me to jump in bed with anyone I'm not in love with.)"

In that relationship as well as the ones to follow, Carrie stayed little girlish. "I didn't take responsibility for me and I let myself get used." This pattern reached its culmination when she got black-balled from a coveted work assignment because the man she'd been sexually involved with didn't want her on the same job with another of his girlfriends. "After that I was a physical and emotional mess. I came home like a wounded animal. I couldn't read, walk, type or sleep."

She found support not in her family but with the parents of her first boyfriend from camp. "His mother had come up to me one day and said, 'I see you taking care of my son all the time. Who takes care of you?' " After that Carrie dreamed of his mother baking her corn muffins once when she needed nurturing. Now, feeling brittle and fragile, she told his mom she had some heavy reconstructing to do. "Why don't you stay here?" was her invitation in response.

As she recovered Carrie began finishing developmental tasks from adolescence. "I was driving in the car with his mom one day and started acting 13, just like it was hormonal. I'd ask, 'How did you meet your husband?' (and giggle); 'What other guys did you go out with?' 'When did you let him kiss you?' 'What's it like to kiss?' I was collecting a whole mess of information and *laughing*. I *never* laughed as a teenager. And I told her I craved chocolate chip cookies so she stopped the car and bought me some. I chomped and didn't close my mouth and all that awful stuff 13-year-olds do.

"Another time I did 'girls on the beach.' While on a trip to Europe I went to the beach in a bathing suit with two girl friends and did what adolescent girls do — talk about boys and sex. We'd look at men and boys and talk about the perfect male body, falling in love, straight out lust, what do you do then, what do you think of . . . and checked out anatomy. I needed to collect data to arrive at my own decisions, instead of my family's or the culture's decisions."

Back at her boyfriend's parents' the next year she did another part to reclaim her power. "If you can't say no, then yes means nothing, she said. I needed to practice not being adaptable, not doing something somebody else wants you to do when you don't want to do it. I wanted the right to have my own life. I walked around their house for almost a week saying no."

Realizing she was still scared of men, Carried joined a therapy group where she "redid the walk in the woods with Mom", this time getting positive messages and changing her decision about men and sex. "The next day my eyesight was better! I realized that isn't only intellectual. If rational logical thinking worked, we'd probably all be fixed by now."

Gradually growing through adolescence again in steps, she returned to 16. "I loped around; I didn't walk. That's part of being gangly and having a body, not being afraid to move like I was at 16. I went out with the girls one night to check out the truck drivers. We talked about masturbation and about dating in the 1970s and 1980s, the pill syndrome and people who jump in the sack with anybody.

"While I was home (at her ex-boyfriend's parents') that time I went to my high school class reunion. I'd brought two dresses to wear but I really wanted to borrow something from his mom. I needed to have something from a mother who was classy enough but not flaunting, a magical item of clothing to make a statement I'd be proud of about how to be a female. Also, I got plenty of reinforcement from them that I could have a healthy, sound relationship with a man if that's what I wanted, not in order to please them, but because I'm worth it and capable of it."

Carrie's back in Boston now, working full time at her legal job. In answering how she'd changed her life she replied, "For one thing I'm feeling not just physically ready to deal with sex, but emotionally

ready too. I have some men friends here and I could not have done
that before. We may have a sexual relationship sometimes, but first of
all we're friends with a minimum of sexual tension. And I'm relaxed
around men. Before I could not relax and that was sure limiting! The
world is 49% male and it was damn hard to make my way through it
without seeing men. I can say no too. When some man's being an
absolute turkey, I have no compulsions at all about taking my leave.
All the existential questions of why I'm alive have dropped away. And
I'm getting back to a basic love — the outdoors."

Carrie's advice to others who may have reconstructing work to do
in adolescence is:

1. The hardest part is being willing; that's the critical difference. It's
   that simple and that hard.
2. Find somebody who's willing to work *with* you. Nobody else
   can fix you, you work together.
3. Confront the past thoroughly. To do that, you need support, an
   environment of loving people so that you don't have to do it
   alone, and nobody's going to leave you.

| C |
| H |
| A |
| P |
| T |
| E |
| R |
| 7 |

Stage Seven: The Power Of Recycling

The wheel is come full circle.

Shakespeare

Summary

This stage has particular significance for those who are age 19 and older.

Affirmations

It's okay for you to be here.
You can still be taken care of.

It's okay for you to move out in the world, to explore and feed
your senses.

It's okay for you to push and test, to find out limits, to say no and
to become separate.

It's okay for you to have your own view of the world, to be who
you are and to test your power.

It's okay for you to learn how to do things your own way and to
have your own morals and methods.

It's okay for you to be sexual, to have a place among grown-ups
and to succeed.

Normal Symptoms

Symptoms can include needing support to decide, "It's okay to be
here" (at this new level); becoming curious and easily distracted;
craving variety; setting boundaries; establishing limits; exploring who
we are and what we can do; learning "how to do it"; arguing;
changing priorities and values; developing sexuality; creating new,
independent support systems; and experiencing more than one stage
at a time.

Deviations

Hurry Up. This means feeling pressure to do things before we're
adequately prepared; giving our power to people who pressure us
and then failing.

Stay Little. This means feeling too distracted to concentrate or
follow through to finish tasks; rebelling instead of planning; resisting
taking on new roles and then failing.

Developing The Power Of Recycling

The transition to this Seventh Stage is a journey back from
complexity to simplicity, from completion to beginning. Our passage
from the end of one cycle to the beginning of another may be a

prolonged labor or a short one, a difficult birth or an easy one, but having drawn our first breath in the new place, our world is as it is for all newborns: intense, vital, vulnerable and full of possibilities.

This is the life we've been preparing for all these years. We're here and mobile, knowledgeable and independent; we know who we are; we are skillful, sexually mature and unified.

Sam

Sam E. was in his early 50s when he developed "a severe case of dissatisfaction. I didn't know what was going on," he said. "But I was restless. I couldn't sleep; food didn't taste good. I lost my appetite for life. I knew a big change was brewing.

(Stage One) "For quite awhile I daydreamed into space and drifted off in the middle of conversations. Finally I took some time off by myself and discovered, 'I don't like where I am anymore!' Oh, our home was okay. My job (as a company accountant) was okay, too. Life was pleasant, but I wanted to really shuffle the deck completely and deal myself a new situation. I searched deep in myself then. I didn't want everybody to uproot themselves (his wife and three teenage children) if I could make a better adjustment where we were, but the truth was I was done living there.

(Stage Two) "When we (his family) talked it over, they weren't happy about it. I needed as much support as I could muster, so I started telling everybody I knew. They were great. They started bringing me articles and magazines with stories and pictures of people and faraway places. Some of them helped me arrange trips and job interviews to go check out the possibilities. Gradually I got clear. I was tired of working with my head. I wanted to work with my hands.

(Stage Three) "I had to take a stand then, especially with the kids. They'd never known a less expensive life, and they'd have been delighted to talk me out of it. But even though I knew it would mean a cut in pay, I wanted to make it work. Then a friend told me about his old place and I decided to go take a look even though it seemed unlikely. It was a rundown old farm, in need of some love and a lot of hard work, but something about it intrigued me. It was a couple of hundred miles from our city; it was pretty as a picture and best of all,

the barn was constructed so that part of it could be used for some kind of shop or business just off the edge of a small town.

(Stage Four) "That was a crisis point for me because I thought, 'Me, a farmer? I've go to be kidding myself. Me the one they always called egghead and bookworm, the intellectual, the theorist? Me, live a life I've never known and manage to make a living at it besides?' I brought everybody I knew out to see it. My wife was intrigued but the kids really surprised me. They said that they might be happy there, especially if it felt right for me. I sat down on the rickety old steps of that farmhouse, pulled them into my arms and we all had a good cry. In our minds, that was the moment we moved in.

(Stage Five) "How to make it work was the next big issue. We talked to real estate agents, businessmen, farmers, craftspeople, school teachers and found out two big facts. First, there was no furniture repair and refinishing business for miles around and second, I could teach accounting part-time in the school while we got the business started. I took the job and we set a date to move.

(Stage Six) "At that point, I went right back to the start with the soul searching, looking at other possibilities, thinking it over and wondering if it was right for me, if I had the skills to make it work and if it would help or hurt our marriage.

"We didn't turn back, though. We had a big farewell party to say goodbye and here we are (new Stage One), living in the country, remodeling the house, gathering eggs from the chickens and refinishing furniture. It has its hard places, but I love it. In fact, we all do."

Carole

Carole S. described her recycling process, "I received a letter informing me I'd just received a job promotion.

(Stage One) "For about a week I felt all quiet inside and like the world was new. I told people about it, but I felt sad and lonely if they said, 'Good for you' unless they touched me, too. I really needed to *feel* that reassurance.

(Stage Two) "I got the manual describing my new job and I entered it in a random way, wondering who wrote it, what they were thinking about and how they knew how to write it. I felt a sense of

awe and wonder mixed with curiosity. I had to feel my way around at work unitl I got used to my new location, the new people and my new responsibilities.

(Stage Three) "I wanted to share my delight with my husband but he gave me the cold shoulder. I kept asking him to at least read my new job description but he didn't, even after I'd asked him several times. I would not be consoled by other people. Finally I set a limit, I wouldn't let him go to a party held in my honor unless he read it. And I decided I didn't need his approval. He read it and he went.

(Stage Four) "I began to worry about who I was going to be after doing this new job awhile. Then, one of my projects came out wrong. Some of the drawings and graphs were placed improperly. I felt absolutely powerless and got into a terrible uproar about it. I even magically tried to wish them away; better gone than wrong, I said. But I weathered that storm and decided to find out what I could do with my new level of power.

(Stage Five) "I got really involved in learning a new role in my professional community. I had to learn a whole lot of new techniques to move into a new project. I had to create a plan for the people I was working with. I had fun doing it and that worked really well.

(Stage Six) "After awhile I began to get fleeting glimpses of a different, older me emerging. I felt like I was in limbo, having to go on about my daily business and somehow inside waiting for that newness to emerge. I started forgetting things and then I started reviewing what had happened so far. I got really scared then, realizing how soon everything would be different. I dredged up all the awful stuff from the past as I attempted to figure out what would happen to me. I was scared people might not love me if I made this change completely or if I stayed the same.

(Stage One) "Now that seems like ancient history. I know I'm different, older and more experienced. I feel content with what I've done, but I know I'm not ready yet. This morning I just lay in bed drinking a hot cup of tea and watching the rain freeze on the trees. It was the highlight of my day, and that's exactly what I need to be doing for now.

"I went through the same stages during grieving and recovering when my mother died. That was a process I had more control over because I could lengthen or shorten it, depending on how much time I had available to say goodbye and let go. So, in relation to my job I'm in Stage One. In relation to my daughter I'm pulled into adolescence and following my mother's death I'm in Stage Five, closing the estate and finding new, older Moms to relate to. It's easier for me to recognize all this as a normal process than it is for my daughter (who's going through it for the first time) because I've been there and know the ropes. That's the wisdom of having done it many times."

The *Power of Recycling* is that we now can use nature's cyclic design as the perfect template for our continued evolution as adults, using each turn to create our life vision as we gather support, add strength and develop our powers.

Knowing these stages, there is no need to be surprised by the progressions of life at their most basic level because we've been here before and no matter what the content is, the ground rules are the same. We still carry out the same developmental tasks, in these grown-up repetitions, even though we finished them in a previous turn.

We profoundly affect our relationships, our feelings of satisfaction and our involvement in the world according to what we decide to do about these tasks in adulthood. By attending to the natural pattern in an awake, intelligent manner, we can live in simplicity and at peace, no matter how complex the outer aspects of our lives may seem. By doing so, we also gain fundamental understanding of and connection with all people and all living things. Supporting that natural growth process in others as we carry out our own tasks, we expose ourselves to possibilities we might not have noticed. And finally, knowing that different things are important at different times, we free ourselves to concentrate on tasks at hand without being burdened about tomorrow's labors.

This seventh stage brings with it the gift of greatly increased capacities for mental life. Energy consumed by growing aspects of ourselves can now be used to produce. The world of adulthood is still a physical one in that it is a scene for action. Through action in accord with our cyclic needs, we maximize that privilege.

Playful experimentation is a key to knowing the possibilities of adult life just as it is in childhood. Even with all our grown-up information and experience, we're still children in a vast and unknown universe of constant change. We're older and taller; we're called grown-ups; we're people granted a seventh power, which gives us the opportunity to use the other six. The entire cycle of life is now our ring of power, the source of our abilities and the wellspring for our actions.

In Stage Seven we need to do the following tasks:

1. Update, revise and carry out our life vision and plan
2. Work with our own stages of growth
3. Develop and maintain the relationships we need for support
4. Find, enter and leave environments in which we can grow in particular ways
5. Maintain our philosophy of life as we learn from experiences
6. Participate, accept and carry out responsibilities
7. Claim our competency in the world of adults
8. Assume new roles in the stages: a child one time and a parent the next; a student one time and a teacher the next
9. Recognize and solve problems of growth, including those from past stages

For the rest of our lives we have the opportunity to develop our *Power of Recycling,* which will work *for* us as long as we do the developmental tasks associated with it.

Cycle Sabotage In Stage Seven

Stage Seven sabotage takes two common forms: (1) failing to carry out the developmental tasks of our current life and (2) not taking care of unfinished business in the previous six stages. Either way, we stay on the same level in the cycle and don't advance. Even if we change our lives in outward form, we still find the same lessons to be learned in the new situation. We may change jobs or locations or partners, become single or couple up, get fired or promoted, but we stay stuck in the same self-defeating patterns because we have not yet aligned ourselves with our own growth and done the work that would finish this level and allow us to move on.

Carole

Carole S. discovered this when she got hung up in the separation process (see Stage Three) after her mother's death. She said, "I was so angry with her that I sabotaged what I was doing at work. I should have been setting up new rules and procedures and changing my priorities, but instead I just resisted doing it."

Jacob

Jacob R., an inventory control officer, got stuck in a Stage One issue. He lost his job and his fiance to another man all within a period of nine months. He was so devastated that he didn't organize himself to look for a job. Instead, he took refuge in the arms of a cuddly, pudgy woman acquaintance of his in a short-lived affair. Finally, some friends found an employment agency who'd tell him what to do, step-by-step. (Thus, he managed to receive symbolically some of the feeding he so craved.) He finally landed and kept another job, but he hasn't let go of his ex-fiance. Rather than carrying out the tasks that would help him let go (forming a new, healthy bond for the infant inside him), he's hanging on, repeating how "it might have been."

One challenge of the recycling stage is to avoid becoming entrapped, fooled or limited by cultural values that go against our cyclic needs. For example, one such pressure is to not have the full range of developmental needs, but only the ones the culture defines as okay. To succumb to this is to invite not only milder discomforts or unpleasantries, but also can lead directly to tissue damage, if sustained. Another such pressure is from cultural values that encourage a division of responsibility based on gender rather than free will and natural ability. These are a disservice to all people because they dictate who does what, rendering unavailable the innate expressiveness and natural talents of all people. Last, cultural time tables about when tasks are to be achieved are often dramatically out of synchronization with the natural learning rhythm of the cycle. To follow cultural dictates in this circumstance is to choose physical and emotional distress and constant inner turmoil.

The emotional box we experience when we're restricting our power potential is a clue to becoming aware of what we need to do to get on with life. Then, having done that work, we see a similar lesson arise and figure it out right away.

Adulthood is about finding our own way, with a maximum of support, encouragement, generosity, guidance and benign neglect. No one else can or will do it for us whether we accept self-responsibility or not.

The powers we can gain from a commitment to our own growth are those that support our own life and the lives of others. The cycle does not grant us the right to use each other, to control and dominate or to rule for material gain or egotistical advantage. Our cyclic birthright grants us the capacity to respond to our own potential and in so doing to encourage, by example and cooperation, the healthy growth of others.

If we've hurried through previous stages to avoid dependency, we may respond to others pushing us to do things before we've carried out the necessary preparation. We need to relax and know that there is enough support when we take the time to arrange it. If we've stayed little, we may "lollygag" around, waiting to get things perfect, get distracted from our tasks and goals or keep responding to people who say they need us instead of doing what we need to do. We need to realize that it's really okay to grow up because we don't have to give up safety or be abandoned.

Stage Seven Games[32]

We may still play games in Stage Seven but if we have stayed on our developmental track and not buried the work we needed to do, they are short-lived and not particularly intense. We may play *Ain't It Awful* for 15 minutes, for example, and then go do something effective about problems. However, when we have sabotaged ourselves by denying needs, our involvement in games is often long, drawn-out and painful, and results in a serious payoff such as a lost job, a broken marriage or a broken body.

Body Language Of Recycling

Experiencing temporary physical symptoms that we recognize as signals and doing something about them is part of normal recycling. We sabotage ourselves when we fail to recognize physical symptoms, when we do nothing about them or even when we aggravate them until they become a disease.

However, we can always use these clues to rewrite our life plan, to reestablish harmony with nature's design or to end our conflict with our nature. When our developmental clock says, "Time for touching or updating our identity; or to deal with sexual issues, to explore or develop independence," we still can decide to do it. And now we have the full range of adult resources at our disposal.

Reclaiming The Power Of Recycling

The following studies are examples of Stage Seven, *The Power of Recycling.*

Bertram

Bertram Samuelson (see Stage Three) discovered, "You can't fix another person because we each have to do our own developmental tasks. You can invite, you can encourage, but they may not want to work on themselves. What you can do is get your act together and hope the other person will do the same.

"I made the decision that I was going to get healthy and wind down on the destructive stuff I was doing. I had to put the effort that was going into trying to change other people into moving toward changing myself. For me, that meant a giant step back in order to prepare myself. I had to make some decisions about how I wanted to spend my time. I asked myself, 'Where will I be if I do it and where will I be if I don't?' I decided I didn't want to wait until my next life to give myself a better start. I wanted to do it now."

Katie

Having decided to resolve the issues that prevented her from moving forward, Katie G. (see Stage Two) needed to find someone to model. "I didn't find the right person standing on any street corner out there," she said. "I needed somebody who had worked through a lot of things in their own life, somebody who was sensitive because they'd been there and knew what it felt like."

Mitch

Mitch Salzman (see Stage One) agreed. "I had to take the risk of finding a relationship I trusted. That was the first step," he said. "If I didn't like what Abdul had, I went to Shazaam. If I didn't like what Shazaam had, I went to Schmeckela. If I felt uptight with the person, I cut out and checked it out with somebody else."

Valerie

Valerie S. (see Stage One) found, ". . . the right people to work with through friends of friends who knew some people and felt satisfied with what happened. That's how I felt good enough about myself to dive to the bottom and come up again. That's what I needed to do. If I wasn't ready, I decided not to push myself," she said. "I needed to go one step at a time as I was ready."

Michael

To learn how to set up a supportive relationship in which he could catch up on his development, Michael G. *(Stage Two)* looked at people he thought were doing a good job and watched what they did. He observed, "They were asking for what they wanted, to be hugged and held or to be listened to for five minutes. I didn't know you could do anything in small amounts of time. So I started asking too. In little bits at first, I found out you really can relearn to meet your needs simply, too, just like babies do. When they're hungry, they cry. It's that basic."

Marcia, Katie, Bill and Mitch

Marcia, Katie, Bill and Mitch met together every other week for over a year to support each other's development. They made agreements at the beginning that were essential protection for their work. "We agreed to solve problems, and not to walk away from them. We can still do it our own way and within a reasonable amount of time," Mitch remembers.

"We had an emergency stop," Katie recalls. "If one person 'blew the whistle' to interrupt for the safety of a relationship, the others agreed to abide by it. We also agreed that when one of us said, 'There's a problem,' the others would give their time and attention to deal with it. We recognized that some matters are worked out in minutes, while others may take months or years."

"Cooperation was important, too," added Marcia. "We agreed that we all have the same basic needs in the developmental stages and that we'd cooperate with each other in meeting those needs."

"Negotiation and cooperation were the ways we'd use to get what we wanted," Bill said. "We agreed not to use threats or violence as a means of getting what we wanted. If anybody wanted to leave the group, we decided to give three meetings' notice. That way we were protected from abandonment when the going got rough."

Susan

Susan B. stressed the importance of having the environment set up well. "When I first started out wanting to be free, I wasn't really free. I was 30 years old, pretending to be free. My body was 30 but the rest of me could be any age I wanted to be. Shedding the years was easy because I was in a room that invited me to be three. It invited me to explore the things three-year-olds explore and do the things they do."

Nancy

Going back to the stage-setting levels of her development, Nancy Johns, along with her family, transformed their home environment both physically and emotionally. "We set up areas for play, places where it would be easy to cuddle or to get someone to hold you," she said. "Now home is a place to let go and grow."

Developmental
Exercises

<table>
<tr><td>

C
H
A
P
T
E
R

1
</td><td>

Creating A Vision
</td></tr>
</table>

Find a nice, comfortable and quiet place to be in and a nice comfortable position and relax. Place next to you a large sheet of blank paper and some colored crayons or pens.

Put aside your life story for just this one moment. To do that, take a minute now to review your day. What was it like? Take a nice, slow, deep breath and let that go. Next go back over the months that have just passed. Recall the friends you saw, the people you met, the celebrations, the gifts and so forth. Then, take another nice deep breath and let that go.

Now, in your imagination, take a step as if you were soaring above your whole life. Go so high above it that you can see the whole of it from the present back to the time when you were born. See that family you were born into, your mother, father, the other children, the place where you were born, the country and the town. Review the experiences you've had in your life up to this point, the kind of infancy you had, the kind of childhood, the schools you went to, the high school you graduated from and how you entered adulthood.

Next, review how you've been living your adult life up to this point, the experiences you've created, the network of friends and people you've associated with, the skills you've developed, your areas of strength and your weak points too.

Then instead of looking back, look to a different world. In this world there are no limitations, no considerations, no can't's. The world of the future, like the piece of paper before you, is blank. Only you can fill it in — no one else. In this world of total possibility, what kind of future do you wish to create?

At this moment picture that you are holding a magic wand in your hand. Get a good grip on it. While you are holding this wand, you can make your life anything you want it to be. Let the power of the wand flow through the colored crayons and onto the blank paper before you.

1. Choose the age you want to be.
2. Choose the place, anywhere in the world, where you live.
3. Now, choose the education you would like to have.
4. Choose the friends you would like to have.
5. Choose any possessions you would like to have. It's all here.
6. How big is your family?
7. What kind of work are you doing, or are you working at all?
8. How much money do you have?
9. What skills do you have?
10. Describe your physical appearance.
11. Describe how you spend your days.
12. Describe your contribution to the world and to society.
13. Take a minute, while you are still holding the wand to finish up your vision. Fill in any other details you want to include.

Now come back to this place.

Finally, reaffirm your vision with the statement: **I deserve all of this and more!**

As you finish up, and when you are ready, put the magic wand in a safe place so you can find it and use it again at any time you need it.

Now that you have described your life as you want to create it, you are ready to integrate it into the stages of your developmental cycle and make it your dream come true.

Developmental Script Questionnaire

Use this section to discover the key elements of your own script developmental plan. Use the information you discover in responding to the questions below to direct you in making your own life vision become a reality, stage by stage.

When you answer the following questions, allow your imagination to flow freely. Write down the *first* response that comes to your mind without worrying about whether or not it is correct. Even if you think you're just making up an answer, write it down. This is not a test; you will not be graded. To aid your memory, respond in the present; that is, say "I am," not "I was." Again use your paper, colored crayons or pen.

Stage One — Being

1. Imagine you are just born. List the people who are interested in your birth.
2. What are their reactions?
3. Imagine you are four months old. You cannot walk or talk, you can only cry. You are hungry and cry to be picked up and fed. What is your mother's reaction?
4. What is your father's reaction?
5. What significant events, if any, happened in the first six months of your life?
6. What conclusions do you reach about who you are and what life is like?

Stage Two — Doing

1. Imagine you are a toddler, just old enough to crawl, but not old enough to control your behavior. Your job developmentally is to do things and to learn about the world by sensing your environment. You need to taste everything, put the world in your mouth and touch all that you see. You are busy doing what toddlers do.
2. What is your mother's reaction?
3. What is your father's reaction?
4. What significant events happened when you were between six and eighteen months old?
5. What conclusions do you reach about doing things and getting support for doing?

Stage Three — Thinking

1. Imagine you are a two-year-old beginning to separate from your infant dependency. You need to say *no*, to test the limits, to be contrary and to learn to think for yourself. What is your father's reaction when he wants you to do something and you assert, *no?*

2. What is your mother's reaction?
3. What significant events happened when you were between eighteen months and three years of age?
4. What conclusions do you reach about whether it's okay to be separate and think for yourself?

Stage Four — Identity

1. Imagine you are between three and six years old. Like children this age, you want to find out what happens if . . . (if I pretend I didn't hear somebody tell me to stop doing something . . . if I steal even though I've been told I may get into trouble). You also want to know *why*, such as, "Why is the sky blue?" or "Why does it get dark outside?" or "Why are there boys and girls?" You love to test your power. You do something your parents told you not to . . . you go into the street, take the cookies out of the cookie jar or dump the plants out of their pots to make a magic forest with them.
2. What is your mother's reaction?
3. What is your father's reaction?
4. What significant events happened during this age?
5. What conclusions do you reach about your power?

Stage Five — Skillfulness

1. Imagine you are between six and twelve years old, and your life is just as it was then. You are developing your own skills. You want to do things your own way. You want to argue and hassle. You are asked to do something, and you argue about it.
2. What is your mother's reaction?
3. What is your father's reaction?
4. What significant events happened when you were between six and twelve years old?
5. What conclusions do you reach about doing things your own way and having your own values?

Stage Six — Regeneration

1. Imagine you are an adolescent, new to the world of sexual urges and longings. You're old enough to be fairly independent, but you're not all grown-up. You still need support and protection. You feel hungry for loving affection and contact with your parents.
2. What is your mother's reaction?
3. What is your father's reaction?
4. What significant events happened when you were an adolescent?
5. What are your conclusions about becoming sexual and growing up?
6. Imagine you are between 16 and 18. You are breaking away from your parents, wanting to finish the emotional bonds through which you have been relating to them as parents instead of people. You have your own world view and it doesn't agree with that of your parents. You insist on making decisions about your life based on your own, not your parents' values.
7. What is your mother's reaction?
8. What is your father's reaction?
9. What conclusions do you reach about separating and finishing growing up?

Stage Seven[33]

1. What is your favorite fairy tale?
2. What is your favorite song?
3. What is your favorite movie?
4. How will you die?
5. Write your own epitaph.
6. What were your parents' favorite sayings about life?
7. What did you want to be when you grew up?
8. What was your childhood nickname?
9. Describe the bad feelings you've had most often in life.

<table>
<tr><td>

C
H
A
P
T
E
R

3
</td><td>

Using The Think
Structure For Creating
Your Personal
Developmental
Affirmations
</td></tr>
</table>

By completing the exercises in this chapter, you will have one personalized affirmation for each stage. Use it to replace limiting decisions you may have discovered in the Developmental Script Questionnaire. Complete both parts of the exercise presented below. The Think Structure will help you organize what motivates or drives you to play games or to develop physical symptoms. Then compose your personal affirmation.

The Think Structure:
A Way To Feel Fine Faster[34]

1. I am _____
                    (feeling)
2. . . . that if I _____
                    (*behavior* I initiate)
3. I will be _____
                    (undesired response)
4. . . . instead of _____
                    (desired response)
5. . . . so I _____
        (ways I avoid this issue and games I play)

Line 1. Use words that a child can understand such as mad (angry) or scared (afraid). A feeling is sad, glad, mad or scared. Words such as anxiety, guilt, remorse, hostility, confusion, etc., are experiences that result from one of the feelings. They go in line 5.

Line 2. Describe what you want to *do*. Say what you *will* do instead of what you will not do. This is a description of how you want to behave, or what you want to do but feel unable to do. Describe this behavior in positive terms; state what you will do rather than what you won't do.

Line 3. This is the response you do *not* want but often get. It is probably the same response you got when you were little, often called the "unhealthy parental response".

Line 4. Write in the responses you want from others instead of the response you get in Line 3. Write the phrases that melt your heart open and make your belly glow with warmth.

Line 5. Write here all the various things you do, the ways you act to cover your feelings in Line 1. This is your list of games and other avoidance mechanisms.

Line 1 or 5? A feeling is your actual body sensation. Sometimes people use feelings as a racket, a psychological smoke screen to prevent the direct expression of a genuine feeling hidden underneath. For example, what appears to be anger may be a smoke screen to cover fear. Likewise, fear can be used to hide anger. Genuine feelings or actual body sensations go in Line 1. Smoke screen feelings or rackets go in Line 5.

Next, you can create your own affirmation by using the responses you gave in Lines 2 and 4 to complete the phrases that follow.

The Affirmation Structures[35]

Think Structure   Your Affirmation

Line 2 _____   becomes   _____
Line 4 _____   becomes   _____

Transforming Script Limitations

To effectively neutralize negative script messages, constantly repeat your affirmations at first. Use many ways to do it; for example, carry them on a small card, on a key ring or in a pocket or purse. One woman for whom spending money is an issue keeps her card in her checkbook. If she begins hassling herself in a store she relates, ". . . to get that check written sooner, or that I'm buying all that junk food for my kids, I read it again." Other people keep a copy near the telephone or on their desk, wherever they will read them frequently.[36] Other suggestions[37] are:

1. Say them to yourself, to the Child in yourself and to your children.
2. Write them over and over.
3. Carry them around and look at them.
4. Put them on the wall in the kitchen, bathroom or bedroom, wherever you will see them frequently.
5. Let other people know what you need to hear and invite them to say it to you.
6. Record them on a tape and play it back to yourself.
7. Repeat them sometimes silently to yourself, sometimes out loud, sometimes when being quiet and sometimes when physically active.
8. Pay attention to your internal thoughts and feelings as you respond to the new message, for these are important clues to the age and stage in which you need to develop your power.

Your needs are okay and it's important to get them met within the limits of the responsibilities you have chosen. You don't have to contrive a conflict between what you need and your responsibilities. They need not conflict. For example, you may need to take some time out, yet you have other commitments. You can find ways to meet responsibilities *and* have time out.

Protection from injury or damage is built into your new message because you are repeating a powerful thought and can decide for yourself how to act. The message is designed to permit your deeper emotions and developmental processes instead of squelching them. In repeating affirming messages, you are already beginning to develop beyond your script limitations.

Again, to remind you, use the messages to direct you as you go through each stage of manifesting your vision. Use the following chapters to assist you in completing the tasks of each stage.

Exercises For
Developing The Power
Of Being

Taking Inventory

I like to carry out the Stage One tasks in the following manner (check your favorite):

_____ 1. While working, to satisfy that urge to suck (by sipping coffee, for example)

_____ 2. Taking a bubble bath

_____ 3. Getting someone else to fix my hair

_____ 4. Having an intimate friend bathe me

_____ 5. Having a massage

_____ 6. Cuddling up with a friend

_____ 7. Enjoying doing absolutely nothing

_____ 8. Wrapping up in blankets

———   9. Hanging in a hammock for hours
———   10. Eating numerous small meals
———   11. Sucking on hard biscuits, etc.
———   12. Taking a steam bath, hot tub or sauna
———   13. Being held
———   14. Taking frequent naps

Receiving Affirmations And Support

The following positive messages affirm the *Power to Be:*

- It's okay for you to be here, to be fed and touched and taken care of.
- You have a right to be here.
- I'm glad you're a (boy-girl).
- Your needs are okay with me.
- I like to be near you and to touch you.
- You don't have to hurry; you can take your time.

On your paper:

1. Write the ways you like others to affirm and support you in Stage I.
2. List the people in your life who give you unconditional support for **Being**.

Caution: There is a significant difference between exploring now and regressing back to being an infant again. Holding is something friends can do with each other. Becoming an infant again through regression is a therapeutic procedure to be used only by those with proper training. It is not for beginners. If you're already doing it, stop. You deserve to have adequate protection. If you need to return to being an infant again, find good well-qualified parents for yourself and establish a contract first. (For further guidelines in setting up a new parenting relationship, see Chapter 10 on Exercises for *Developing the Power of Recycling.*)

Being Held

Holding is a direct, basic way to provide support to anyone at any age. It's fine for grown-ups of any age to ask to be held.[38] Meeting

Stage One needs means working directly with the sustaining systems of the body through feeding and physical touching. When you ask someone to hold you, establish a time limit first. Then you can relax completely and let your friend tell you when the time is up.

Gather several pillows and a blanket to have nearby for supporting a comfortable position and put a blanket within your friend's easy reach because you may cool down considerably as your muscle tension decreases. Go to the bathroom before being held, because a full bladder or colon will be an unwelcome interruption.

Let your friend find a comfortable position with good back support. Put a few pillows under the arm that will hold your head, and also next to your friend's leg so that your pelvis can rest on them and not cut off circulation.

Your friend should hold you with the *least* physical tension so that you'll be able to relax. If he or she is tense, you may begin doubting his or her motivation to hold you. Regardless of the cause, tension is picked up as resistance to holding and may remind you of lack of love when you were young. A relaxed, open body transfers energy easily and feeds both people.

When your friend is ready, sit down on the pillows next to his or her leg. Lie down across the lap, resting your head on the opposite arm. Don't lean on your elbow, but keep your arms next to your chest. Don't put your other arm around your caretaker, let the holder hold you. Draw your knees up, too; then relax and let go. From here on, others can take care of you.

Even if you visit the bathroom, you may need to go again soon after being held. Your body may flush away fluids that were retained by muscle tension and released during the relaxation of being held.

If you have competition issues to work out, you may find significance in being held when someone else is held. You may need to find out — at this most basic level — there *really* is enough for everybody.

Allow enough time at the end for you and the person holding you to get up slowly, stretch, walk around and share experiences with each other. You may want to sit next to each other a little while and continue touching. Remember that you may want to be in touch again. You can make those plans now.

Giving Affirmations And Support

There are many ways to give Stage One affirming messages. For example, to a guest . . . "I'm glad you're here, (name). Think of this house as your house." "I like to sit next to you when we're talking." "I'm glad you're a girl, too, so we can have plenty of girl talk. There's enough time for us to play and work, so we don't have to hurry."

On your paper:

1. Make a list of the ways you like to affirm others who are growing through Stage One.
2. Make a list of the ways you like to take care of other people when they're in Stage One.

Holding Someone

Most people think being held is preferable to holding. You may be surprised to find your "batteries" are recharged by holding as well as by being held. Two people in close contact share the same energy field, feeding, calming and soothing both of you.

People being held sometimes tense up or draw their face away from contact with another's breast area because of a fear of genital feelings. You can make a statement such as, "I'm not afraid of your being close to my breast," or "I'm not afraid of feeling good over having genital feelings."

Everyone has genital feelings. During stress we release adrenalin into our bloodstream, decrease circulation to sex organs and send blood to our muscles so that we can defend ourselves. When being held, our bodies relax and the blood returns to our sex organs. We may feel this as a rush of sexual energy when being held or holding someone else. Reaffirm to yourself and the person you're holding that this is about nurturing, not sexuality.

Close contact between one person's mouth and another's chest stimulates the release of hormones similar to ones in the blood of nursing mothers. Both men and women have this natural reaction, which results in a brief surge of genital feelings. This is a normal reaction to be expected and is nothing to fear.

When holding someone, notice how you're feeling. If you're frightened or tense, say so. Think about whether you're willing to continue. If not, tell the person you're not ready to continue because you need to deal with your feelings before you can relax.

You may want to have other people provide support, too. Ask them to press or lightly touch any hard, firm, tense places or to lightly brush their fingers along the skin of the feet, legs, face, stomach or back of you or the person you are holding. They can add nice touches of their own, such as a cool washcloth or a lilting lullaby. Unless they feel sleepy, people being held often love to giggle, coo, laugh and play peek-a-boo. They may also feel scared that you're not taking them seriously, that you're laughing at them or that they will be expected to perform. Be sensitive to this possibility and proceed slowly. You can let them know they don't have to adapt by acting cute or smart to get taken care of, but that it's okay to be the way they feel. You may want to take their hands and touch your face with their hands so that they can learn by feeling you're real.

Everybody takes greater risks and feels more willing to change in an atmosphere of abundant praise and positive recognition. When you're hungry, you have little energy to devote to changing. What kind of attention do you need? As for what you want. Feel free to refuse recognition you don't want.

Some examples are:

"How about a hug?"

"Give me a kiss, will you?"

"Let's hold hands."

"Will you put your arm around me? That feels so good."

"I don't like to be slapped (tickled, pinched or teased)."

"Tell me what you like best about me."

"I'm not going to accept that I'm (ugly, mean, selfish or stupid)."

Remember that if you're working with either of the first two stages of development, you may resist doing what you need to do unless you have frequent affectionate physical contact available. You don't have to work it all out first. You can get your Stage One needs met *now* and work out problems at your leisure.

You can make significant changes by actively using the affirming messages for Stage One. When you're using the affirmations and meeting your needs by doing the developmental tasks for Stage One and you're still having problems, you may need to work in another stage.

<table>
<tr><td>

C
H
A
P
T
E
R

5
</td><td>

Exercises For
Developing The Power
Of Doing
</td></tr>
</table>

Taking Inventory

I like to carry out Stage Two tasks in the following manner by (check your favorites):

_____ 1. Gnawing, chewing or sinking my teeth into something
_____ 2. Developing a short attention span and becoming easily distracted
_____ 3. Skipping from one project to another
_____ 4. Being fascinated by colors
_____ 5. Listening to different sounds
_____ 6. Looking at different shapes and feeling different textures
_____ 7. Going to the local coffee shop to people-watch and talk to some of them

——— 8. Taking a long walk to no place in particular, especially holding hands with a friend

——— 9. Eating crunchy, chewy foods like popcorn, steak bones or raw vegetables

——— 10. Wearing bright colors, and making noises with musical instruments, silverware, pots and pans just to hear the noises

——— 11. Making a long visit to the kiddie park to swing on the swing, play in the sand and be one of the kids

——— 12. Going somewhere I've never been before, especially to have a friend take me there

——— 13. Enjoying the smells in the world, such as roses, lilies, daffodils, tomatoes, cherries, onions or garlic

Receiving Affirmations And Support

The following affirming messages affirm the *Power of Doing:*

- It's okay for you to move out in the world, to explore, to feel your senses and be taken care of.
- It's okay to explore and experiment.
- You can do things and get support at the same time.
- It's okay for you to initiate.
- You can be curious and intuitive.
- You can get attention or approval and still act the way you really feel.

On a separate paper:

1. Write the ways you like others to affirm and support you in Stage Two.
2. List the people in your life who offer unconditional support for **Doing**.

Caution: There is a big difference between exploring in the present moment and regressing to the toddler stage. The latter requires appropriate protection. Reread the caution on page 164. It applies to all the stages.

Exploring

What would you like to do that you've never done before? Would you like to go somewhere that you've never been, relate to other people in a way you never have or try a new activity? Would you like to explore the city or the country, a bookstore or a bowling alley, a campground or a corner store? Decide what you'd like to do. On your paper write the following.

1. I would like to:

   Who would you like to do it with? Pick someone you know who knows this place or activity well, someone you really like to be with and with whom you'll feel safe. Ask her to introduce you, to show you around in this new territory so that you can see it with your own eyes but with guidance and protection.

2. I would like to do this with:

   Arrange a time and do it together. Remember that in the fun and excitement of having your friend's support in a novel experience, you may experience a great deal of exuberance and excitement. Don't be carried away by it. Just because you never knew that violins or guitars or old books or camping could be so fantastic, that doesn't mean you should immediately buy a violin or a campground or even camping equipment. Check it out with your friend before you get so involved; his or her benign opinion is part of your protection.

Giving Affirmations And Support

There are many ways to give Stage Two affirming messages. For example, to a friend say, "That's a fine creation (paper airplane, painting or layer cake)." "Come on. I'll take you out to the swimming hole and we'll take a picnic." "We've worked long enough. Let's go find a place we've never been before. We can be back in an hour." "Go ahead and take the day off. You don't have to be sick. You can just go fishing." "It's okay to get a baby-sitter and take a nap or go wandering." "Feel free to call me if you want to touch base. You can interrupt me for a few minutes."

On your blank paper:

1. Make a list of the ways you like to affirm others who are growing through Stage Two.
2. Make a list of the ways you like to support other people when they are developing their *Power of Doing.*

Supporting Others In Exploring

If you are going to support someone else's explorations, keep in mind that explorers of any age have a tremendously short attention span. Their job is to learn about a new part of the world, some portion they've never known before. In discovering this world, they'll discover themselves anew. Your job is to provide a maximum of variety with a minimum of required concentration.

Explorers need short bouts of physical contact and expressions of affection in between their forays off into the unknown, new world. Plan for these moments to ensure that everything goes smoothly.

Make sure the explorer is supervised at all times. In other words, make sure you know what they're doing and check out the dangers for yourself. They are new to this world and don't know what the dangers are; that's why they've engaged your protection.

Even grown-up explorers with their voracious appetite for something new and different can get over stimulated. Plan frequent rest periods and snack times, and if they seem irritable, reduce the level of new input down to a level they can handle. While they rest, they need closeness and intimacy.

After the exploration is over, plan some time to talk about what happened. And remember to give them affirming messages about what they did. Then plan a time for you to explore. That's a great way to recover!

If you think you may have an exploratory problem to work out, here is some advice from Katie (see Part Two, Stage Two): "You can make changes if you're 38 or 68. You don't have to be any particular age to be exploratory. Also, thinking is not part of this stage; it's part of the next one. You'll get back into thinking soon enough after you've given yourself enough sensory knowledge, such as seeing, tasting, touching, smelling and moving through the world. Don't worry about not remembering things in this stage.

"A lot of self-help articles about how to change your life guide you to set a goal and then work toward it. That's rampant in women's liberation. My experience in the beginning of the exploratory stage is that I need to *not* establish a goal. If you're in Stage Two, you won't want to do it, nor should you. You don't have to be that old before you're that young. Don't make having a goal just another 'should' in your life. This is such a goal-directed society, don't put yourself down for not having a goal. And remember the big one — get support."

Remember, too, that physical touch remains a primary need in this stage. In addition to working with your sensory and motor systems, as well as feeding your eyes, ears, nose and mouth and developing your ability to move, you may want to turn back to the end of Stage One to review touching needs and how to meet them.

Physical touch provides a bridge between feelings and actions. If your feelings and behavior are at odds, you may need to increase your level of physical affection.

You can make significant changes by actively using the affirming messages for Stage Two. If you're still having problems when you're using these messages and meeting your needs by doing the developmental tasks for Stage Two, you may need to work in another stage or you may need to work at a previous younger age.

<table>
<tr><td>C
H
A
P
T
E
R
6</td><td># Exercises For Developing The Power Of Thinking</td></tr>
</table>

Taking Inventory

I like to carry out Stage Three tasks in the following manner by (check your favorites):

_____ 1. Not keeping agreements to see what happens
_____ 2. Spending more money than my budget permits
_____ 3. Not taking care of myself
_____ 4. Complaining when others refuse to do things for me
_____ 5. Saying no, even if I mean yes
_____ 6. Changing my mind every few minutes
_____ 7. Responding angrily to people who confront me

Now, add your personal favorites.

Receiving Affirmations And Support

The following positive messages affirm the *Power To Think:*

- It's okay for you to push and test, to find out limits, to say no and to become separate from me.
- You can think for yourself; you don't have to take care of other people by thinking for them.
- You don't have to be uncertain; you can be sure about what you need.
- You can think about your feelings, and you can feel about your thinking.
- You can let people know when you feel angry.
- I'm glad you're growing up.

On a separate paper:

1. Write the ways you like others to affirm and support you as you carry out Stage Three tasks.
2. Make a list of the people in your life who offer you unconditional support for thinking.

Caution: The remarks made in the previous two chapters apply here also. Do remember that appropriate protection is essential.

Establishing Boundaries[39]

We help each other move from dependence to independence by keeping lines of responsibility clear. Remember that *people* are responsible for behavior: things and situations are not responsible for behavior. To be responsible for yourself and to let others be responsible for themselves, ask questions instead of making statements such as "Will you give me a ride?" instead of "I need a ride (hint, hint)."

Invite others to tell you how they think and feel rather than suggesting how they think or feel. For example, "You will hate this project" encourages negative feelings, whereas "Tell me how you feel about this project" leaves room for all experiences.

You can say no when you need to, out loud, straight, instead of hedging.

A Structure For Thinking

To check out how you think about something ask yourself:

"How do I feel about this?"
"What are the facts?"
"How do I think about this?"
"What's my opinion on this?"

If you need to develop language to describe your feelings, for the next week, three times a day, tell someone else if you are feeling scared, sad, mad or glad. At the end of the week, report what you found out in this experiment.

If you need to separate and become independent, for each person who is important to you, write on one side of a blank card five times when you've felt angry with that person (even little tiny angry feelings). On the other side of the card, describe a gift you'd like to give that person. (You can give the Eiffel Tower or the Brooklyn Bridge, because you'll only write it, not deliver it.) As a third option, if the other person is willing, you may want to give the card to the person and say what you found out in this exercise.

If you believe you have to compete for attention and want to find out how important you are, for each person who's important to you, write five times when you were more important than they were; when you were less important; and, when you were just as important.

Learning To Set Limits

- You don't have to give in to unreasonable demands.
- You don't have to be nice and go that extra mile. That only delays establishing boundaries.
- You can get stroking in other relationships. You don't have to stay in a dependency relationship when you no longer need it.
- Getting your needs met helps you not to wilt and become a pushover when someone is testing you.
- Another person may need to stop stroking you to find out what they can control. You don't have to take it personally or think there's something wrong with you.

Remember, there are no *perfect* limits, only who you are and how you feel. Pay attention to your feelings, and start from there. Your responsibility is to be clear about what you will and will not tolerate. You have a right to exist, to feel what you feel and to take care of yourself by setting limits that are right for you. Handle the first minor infractions right away so that they don't have a chance to grow into major ones. You can have fun, maintain a loving bond *and* have your limits.

Focus on taking care of your own needs and being open and receptive to the other person's needs rather than insisting on conformity. Work *with* resistance instead of attempting to overpower it.

Giving Affirmations And Support

There are many ways to give Stage Three affirming messages. For example, to a spouse say, "I'm glad you want different things than I do. That makes our relationship more interesting." "It's okay with me that you have your own friends. We need to have lives of our own as well as a life together." "I know you're angry now that you've told me. I don't blame you." "I know you want me to figure out what you're feeling without telling me. I'm not a mind reader, and I want you to tell me what's going on with you when you're ready." "Let's go to the beach and play in the sand. We can make sand castles and gooey sand pies!"

On your paper:

1. Make a list of the ways you like to affirm others who are growing through Stage Three.
2. Make a list of the ways you like to support other people when they are in Stage Three.

Aiding Others In Establishing Limits

People can support each other's mutual independence in a warm, loving way by confronting[40] each other, such as bringing each other face to face with feelings, issues and options. Confrontation is a way of saying, "This is important" and "You are important." Guidelines you can use follow.

When you confront you can:

- Keep your goal in mind — think about how you want this situation to end.
- Ask yourself whether or not confronting will be consistent with this goal.
- Decide what level of confrontation is best for the situation.
- Don't reward nonproblem solving by giving lots of strokes, even if they're given while confronting.
- Say you are aware there is a problem and you want to find a solution so that you won't be picked up as just another complaining person.
- Evaluate the person's history and the kind of follow up that is available.
- If confrontation doesn't work: (1) find out why so that you can use this information the next time or (2) do something to deescalate the situation, such as telling the person you are going to stop short of solving the problem for now.

When you are being confronted by another person:

- Choose problem solving options.
- Get in touch with your own feelings.
- Check out how others feel about your behavior.
- Think about what you *can* do.
- Ask others what they think can be done.
- Find out what others feel you *should* do.

Think about what you feel you should do. Then you are ready to choose what you are *going* to do.

If you think you may have power potential to reclaim in Stage Three, remember:

- You may need to establish a new dependency relationship as a first step.
- You don't have to do it according to somebody else's standards or do it right to please others.
- Go ahead and *feel* your anger. You may need to stamp your feet so that you can be done with it. It's only a feeling.
- You can learn from other people who handle anger well.

- Say so when you need to crab and fuss so that you can invite others to be sympathetic listeners.
- Accept that you don't have to be liked all the time. Some flack and dissonance *is* part of living.
- Information is power — the power to think. Don't starve for knowledge. When you need to know something, ask.
- Time is necessary to grow out of dependency and to integrate new information. You don't have to hurry.
- Growing beyond a dependency relationship can seem to be a huge task when only two people are involved. You may each need to relate to other people for a while. That way you can have separate experiences.

You can make significant changes by actively using the affirming messages for Stage Three. If you are still having problems when you're using these messages and meeting your current needs by doing the developmental tasks for this stage, you may need to work in another stage or you may need to work at a previous, younger age.

Treats For Two-Year-Olds Of Any Age[41]

Two-year-olds of any chronological age may be contrary but they are also fun loving and appreciate activities tailored to their developmental stage. When working out separation issues, all the brilliant analysis in the world can't make up for a couple of hours playing in a sandpile, a mud hole or a newspapered room with lots of play dough. Some people satisfy these urges by making bread, which requires a lot of hand-kneading. Although this is fine, it is limited by the product at the end of the process. Messing just to mess, not to produce something, can excite glee from the most serious adult, after only a few minutes of saying, "Surely not *me* playing with all that goop!"

At one weekend group, the grown-up "two-year-olds" were treated to a 15-foot wide mud hole that had been roped off in a small orchard in which the hosts had run water for two days. When people are free to mess in such direct and satisfying ways, they need not carry the urge to mess into other areas of life. The following are some recipes:

Cloud dough uses 6 cups flour to 1 cup salad oil. Add enough water to make dough soft and pliable. This is easy for two-year-olds to use. Add food coloring with water for smooth colors, or with dough mixture for a marbled effect.

Play dough uses 2 cup flour to 1 cup salt. (Add 1 tablespoon powdered alum if you want to keep the dough.) Add to the dry mixture 1 cup hot water with 1 tablespoon salad oil and food coloring, if desired. Add water if flour doesn't mix and is too sticky.

Clay dough uses 6 cups flour to 6 cups salt plus 6 tablespoons powdered alum. Add a little water at a time until the consistency of clay is reached. Stir first and later use hands. If the dough is too sticky, add flour and salt in equal portions. To store, place fist-sized balls in a covered container. Wrap balls in damp cloth and keep damp.

Finger paints are made from 2 parts powdered tempera to one part flaked soap *or* one part liquid detergent to two parts liquid tempera.

Finger paints (especially recommended) are made from bar soap pieces grated as you would do to cheese. Then mix the soap with water to make a "goopey" consistency. Let the mixture set a few days or as long as you like. When ready to use, scoop out a cup of goop and sprinkle in a tablespoon of tempera. Beat with an electric mixer. This has the texture of whipping cream and cleans from skin and clothes like a dream. It's great for body painting.

<table>
<tr><td>C
H
A
P
T
E
R

7</td><td># Exercises For
Developing The Power
Of Identity</td></tr>
</table>

Taking Inventory

I like to carry out the tasks of Stage Four and find out how I can affect myself and other people by (check your favorites):

_____ 1. Setting up disagreements between them
_____ 2. Getting sick (eating too much candy, for example)
_____ 3. Telling a fantasy as if it were fact
_____ 4. Taking things that don't belong to me
_____ 5. Getting involved in a political struggle
_____ 6. Dividing or matchmaking friends

Now, write your personal favorites.

When I'm developing my *Power of Indentity*, I:

1. Deal with conflicts by _____
2. Find out what it means to be a man or woman by _____
3. Fantasize or have nightmares about _____

Your ability to affect others is directly related to your supply of attention, affection and nurturing. Don't rob yourself of the energy from which power is made. Remember, too, that you are not *bad* — testing actively and finding out what happens *if* — are necessary and natural in this stage.

Receiving Affirmations And Support

The following positive messages affirm the *Power of Identity:*

- It's okay for you to have your own view of the world, to be who you are and to test your power.
- It's okay to imagine things without being afraid you'll make them come true.
- You don't have to act scary, sick, sad or mad to get taken care of.
- You can be powerful and still have needs.
- It's okay to find out the consequences of your own behavior.
- It's okay for you to explore who you are. It's important for you to find out what you're about.

On a blank sheet of paper:

1. Write the ways you like others to act toward you when you are testing your power in Stage Four.
2. List the people in your life who offer you unconditional support for developing your own power and identity.

Caution: The remarks made about protection for the preceding stages apply in Stage Four also. (Check back to the Stage One exercises.)

Testing Power Safely With Peers

Playing with others is one of the most effective ways to develop identity and self-nurturing. Just as children age three to six, as a grown-up creating an identity, you need to explore the world outside your primary family and play with peers who are important motivators for you.

Because identity is based on gender, you may become actively interested in male and female genitals and may need to find safe, protected ways to see naked bodies. Pictures in books designed for that purpose or experiences with friends, where people can share and resolve feelings are possible solutions.

Remember to include the following ingredients when you're developing your *Power of Identity:*

1. **Caring.** Cultivate affectionate relationships.
2. **Contact.** Develop it with supportive people who want you to nurture yourself.
3. **Protection.** Include professional support if you need it. Grown-ups, as children do in this stage, may invent imaginary playmates or blame others as a way of signaling a need for protection from their own unacceptable impulses. If you're fantasizing monsters, assume you need support from others, and get it.
4. **Reassurance.** Greet your dreams with a welcoming attitude. A resurgence of scary dream material is characteristic of this stage.
5. **To Find Out What Happens.** If you tell a lie or refuse to take responsibility for something you know you did, use that as a starting place or a stepping-stone to working out the issue you're testing.

An "Exorcise" (for learning about your demon)

- Think about and list the ways you negate others or yourself.
- List 20 times when you began to negate yourself. Write down what happened just before that. What were you feeling?
- For each time on the list above, state three options you could use if that situation were to occur again.
- State how old you feel (not how old you are).
- What other ways can you protect your inner child?
- List all the characters you know — real people or characters in plays and books, mythological people, plants or animals — whom you imagine carry these same negative patterns.

- The next time you begin to negate yourself or someone else, substitute one of the affirmations in this chapter. Then check out how you feel.
- Now list all the characters you know who embody positive patterns.
- What do you need to do to make the desirable patterns you've named part of your identity now?

Releasing The Old Identity

When you rework your identity you dismantle complex energy systems. Feeling temporarily fragmented, experiencing rapidly alternating highs and lows of energy and feeling sick or like you are "going crazy", are common aftermaths.

This is a giant step forward, not a giant step backward. Your body is ridding itself of the toxic effects of a limiting identity. Manifestation of such symptoms is a sign of solution (a fact known in Oriental medicine for thousands of years).

Guidelines For Release[42]

- Understand what's happening so that you don't feel victimized. If you suffer about the suffering coming out, in effect you're fighting the release.
- Let your body tell you when the discharging is over. If you want to run the four-minute mile, wait until you've recovered.
- Make arrangements for support right away, especially in the form of contact with those who support your identity change.
- Physical contact (being held or having a massage) will aid the process.
- Drink lots of water so wastes can flush through your kidneys. If you feel nauseated, flush your stomach with water.
- Diet is important. Some people need more food; some need to fast. Listen to what your body tells you.
- This temporary condition is part of the fundamental integrity of your body.

How long does it take to become comfortable with a new identity? Put your hands together, fingers intertwined as if you were about to pray. Notice which finger is on the bottom. Now switch, placing the hands so that the other finger is on the bottom. How long will it take for you to automatically fold your hands with the other finger on the bottom, so that feels comfortable and natural?

Affirming And Supporting Others In Stage Four

There are many ways to give affirming messages to a friend. For example, Susan's husband affirmed her right to know who she is when he agreed to move so that she could search for her mother. A woman was supported in testing her power when she prepared a speech, while her friends answered her telephone. A man lobbying for legislative changes in his community received many messages to take care of his dependency needs and got plenty of support while he was being powerful. A boy in school was affirmed by his teacher when the boy admitted he didn't do his homework and was prepared to deal with the consequences.

On a separate piece of paper:

1. Make a list of the ways you like to affirm others in Stage Four.
2. List the ways you like to support other people when they are developing their *Power of Identity.*

Supporting Others Who Are Testing Power

Any kind of attention, positive *or* negative, reinforces behavior. When someone you know takes something that's yours, for example, remember that this is not a time for lectures about the right to private property. Nor is it a time for scare tactics such as saying "The police will come and haul you away to jail." Saying, "Oh, it's just a stage" discounts testing by pretending it didn't happen or by overlooking it. Let the person experience his or her behavior as his or her own problem. Keep your involvement at an absolute minimum. Also, if you find yourself wanting to fight with someone, look around. Somebody's testing power. Don't let that person control your relationships.

Remember, this person is not really out to get you, but only to see what happens. *You do not have to comply by feeling victimized.* It's a service — it calls your attention to the unresolved differences in your relationships. You can use the opportunity to see what is unresolved, then go ahead and resolve it. Don't accept messages thirdhand. Insist on direct communication.

If you think you have a problem to work out from your first Stage Four, just remember that you can make significant changes by actively using the affirmations for this Stage. If you're still having problems when you're using the affirmations and meeting your current needs by doing the developmental tasks for Stage Four, you may need to work in another Stage or you may need to work at a previous, younger age.

```
C
H
A        Exercises For
P   Developing The Power
T      Of Being Skillful
E
R

8
```

Taking Inventory

I like to carry out the tasks of Stage Five in the following manner
(check your favorites):

_____ 1. Resisting argument
_____ 2. Arguing freely
_____ 3. Exploring the ways others do things
_____ 4. Insisting others do things my way
_____ 5. Checking out new social roles

Now, add your favorites.

Receiving Affirmations And Support

These are positive messages that affirm the *Power of Being Skillful*:

- It's okay to learn how to do things your own way and to have your own morals and methods.
- You don't have to suffer to get what you need.
- You can do it your way.
- You can think before you make that your way.
- It's okay to disagree.
- Trust your feelings to guide you.

On your paper:

1. Write the ways you like others to support you in Stage Five.
2. List the people in your life who offer you unconditional support while you are developing your skills.

Caution: Recall the precautions for previous stages that apply here also. (Review them in the Stage One Exercises).

Creating Structures

- List the skills and values you now have that you want to keep.
- List those you want to change.
- List new ones as you learn them. (Remember, adequate structures include *both* needs and feelings.)

Developing New Skills Or Values

- You can find new ways to do things without giving up accountability.
- The ability to fantasize is central to the ability to create your own methods. However, structures that work well are also created from action with that which you can see, hear, taste, touch or smell. Involve yourself in actions rather than heady conversations. Don't just talk about it, do it!
- Make sure the methods you create allow both goal-oriented and nongoal-oriented exploring. Both are essential to health.
- Leave space to update your skills.

- You can learn to enjoy and value time alone as well as social time. You can learn to structure your time the way you want it to be.
- Find out how other people structure their diet and food intake, decide how you want to feed yourself and learn to prepare foods that are good for you. Providing yourself with adequate nutrition is a basic skill on which other forms of skillfulness depend.
- Learn how to change your stroking diet to be in accordance with your needs, especially by learning how to ask for what you want and refusing what you don't want.
- Learning a physical skill may be a key to change. Women often need to develop strength whereas men may need to refine motor skills and sensitivity.
- You can get support, but develop your own skills. Advice from others is fine, but you need to learn how by doing it yourself.
- If you disapprove of something, say so. The point is to share your values with others, not to show how liberal and free you are.

Friendships With Peers In Stage Five

In Stage Five we especially need to relate to other people who are developing their *Power of Being Skillful*. In creating and maintaining these friendships and loyalties, we learn to survive socially.

How To Assess Your Social Needs

- List three activities you like to do for fun with others.
- List three activities you like to do for fun by yourself.
- Think about a person of the same sex whom you experience as older and wiser. Do you need that person's guidance as you sort out your values?
- How can you better organize your life to meet your social needs?
- What social connections are you no longer motivated to maintain? What do you want to do about them?
- Satisfying relationships are the result of mutual exchanges. When you give more or get more, what can you do to balance the situation?

Sex Roles And Sexuality[43]

We need to actively seek and receive support when changing our cultural values, especially those involving sex roles and sexuality. To change sex roles is to change the way we relate to our family and to society. For a woman this may mean securing training or an education and getting a paying job or keeping a job she already has while her family shares household responsibilities. For a man it may mean taking a different job that gives more emotional satisfaction and contact with his family, or becoming self-employed or even unemployed in order to develop personal talents.

Boys learn from other males how a boy functions and girls learn from females. Role playing, such as asking, "If I'm a girl, how do I have sex?", is common to learn how to assume the skills necessary for growing up. Exploration of this kind is preparation for the sexual changes of adolescence.

Fear Of Being Skillful

We may go through a temporary phase of nightmarish fear just before using new skills. It's as if we're scared that we're going to die if we activate our own structures. Such fear may be about finishing this stage and moving into Stage Six with its sexual issues. We may hide new abilities instead of using them because we don't understand that we don't have to lose anything by doing things effectively.

The point of the work in Stage Five is to open up our system of values so that we can update them naturally and spontaneously while we learn new skills. The old ways become optional whereas the new ones increase our capabilities.

A play group with a leader to provide protection is an excellent method for building skills and values in Stage Five.[44] Each participant can bring a costume or two, thus contributing to the play. Members can play dress-up and have a great time trying on social roles in this peer group setting. Another option is a slumber party where participants can bring sleeping bags plus food to share. Again, protection in the form of a leader is important for support and security.

Giving Affirmations And Support

There are many ways to give Stage Five affirming messages. For example, Danny's father affirmed his son's right to do things his own way when he showed his son how to use a power saw while standing nearby to check for safety. Jane affirmed her friend's right to disagree when they each had a different opinion on abortion. Jane kept her own position while understanding that of her friend. Bill affirmed an employee's right to trust his own feelings as a guide by discussing a policy with the employee, even though the employee was uncomfortable about it.

On your paper:

1. Make a list of the ways you like to affirm others in Stage Five.
2. List the ways you like to give support to others when they are developing the *Power of Being Skillful.*

You can make significant changes by actively using the affirming messages for Stage Five. If you're still having problems when you're using the affirmations and meeting your needs by doing Stage Five developmental tasks, you may need to work at a previous, younger age.

Exercises For Developing The Power Of Regeneration

Taking Inventory

On a separate paper, complete the following statements.
When I'm developing my *Power of Regeneration:*

1. I respond to my dependency needs by _____
2. I respond to my renewed sexual feelings by _____
3. I react to my need for support around sexuality by _____
4. I begin the process of ending a parent or mentor relationship
   by _____
5. I develop my personal view of life by _____

Receiving Affirmations And Support

These messages affirm the *Power of Regeneration:*

- It's okay for you to be sexual, to have a place among grown-ups and to succeed.
- It's okay to be responsible for your own needs, feelings and behavior. You can be a sexual person and still have needs.
- It's okay to be on your own. My love goes with you. You're welcome to come home again.

On blank paper:

1. Write the ways you like others to affirm and support you in your journey through Stage Six.
2. List the people in your life now who offer you unconditional support for regeneration.

Caution: Remember the same precautions that apply for previous stages apply here also. Get adequate protection.

Integrating Being And Sexuality

It's In The Intent. What makes contact "sexual" or "nurturing" is the intent of the parties involved.

You're Never Too Old. You can continue your need for touching and affection and still grow up. Give yourself plenty of time to develop supportive relationships both inside and outside your family.

Touching Leads To Stability. The turbulence of adolescence is the result of rapid physical and hormonal changes. The most effective way to stabilize these changes is physical contact.

Body Pleasure Is Healthy. Learning to be sensually oriented rather than task oriented is a major step in sexual liberation. Pleasuring and being pleasured not only feels good, it is an antidote to many physical and emotional problems.

Groom Without Guilt. If you look good, you invite positive attention. The process of grooming also helps satisfy your need for affection. Go ahead and spend hours on your looks. You can even get together with friends for sessions. There's no need to feel guilty; just don't forget your other responsibilities.

Bodies Don't Lie. If you reexperience growing pains and acne, increase your physical contact. If you're gaining weight, physical touch may help you feel safe enough to deal with whatever issues you need to.

Feelings And Actions Are Separate. If you *feel* sexual it does *not* follow that you need to act on it. Enjoy your feelings whatever they are. You can decide what else you want to do about them, if anything.

Sex With Peers, Not Parents. Enjoy good feelings when you're hugging your parents or your children, but keep sexual gratification out of parenting relationships.

Clarify. Clarify when you want sex and when you want nurturing. If you use one to handle the other you may satisfy neither one.

Work With Your Messages. You may be inhibiting your need for physical and emotional affection with messages that confuse touching and sexuality. Use your time in Stage Six to become aware of them and change them.

You're Not Responsible For Other People's Garbage. You can't prevent others from misinterpreting your intentions. Your responsibility is simply to send clear, straight messages.

Integrating Sexuality And The Power Of Doing

The opportunity to develop your *Power of Doing* and integrate sexuality is often signaled by heightened sensory feelings, teething pain, a short attention span and/or boundless curiosity. You may bounce from one relationship to another, feeding your senses and getting to know what the world has to offer, especially the new world of sexuality. You may want to make variety the spice of your life. Your intuition may be at a peak now, so let senses, rather than thoughts, guide your exploration. You can:

1. **Give up goal orientation at appropriate times** and tune into the world of sounds, colors, shapes, textures, smells and light. You can go for a walk to nowhere in particular, smell the flowers and revel in the shadows and the coolness of the grass. Not wanting to concentrate is only temporary and a normal part of this stage. Let your mind roam; soon enough you'll concentrate again.

2. **Get protection from someone else** while you explore. You'll develop your *Power of Doing* by being able to touch base frequently and being able to hear from the other person that your exploring is important and healthy.
3. **You can use this return** to work out exploratory issues from the first time around and thus reclaim aspects of your *Power of Doing.* You may need to literally get down on the ground. Thinking about it or using your mind doesn't work. You can feed your senses at whatever level you need to. (See Stage Two for techniques.)
4. **Do it!** Renew, feed and sharpen your senses.

Integrating Sexuality With Independence And The Power Of Thinking

During this stage you have easy access to decisions you made at age two when you first began to establish yourself as a separate individual and wanted to think for yourself. In this older return, you can change, add to or update your thinking decision and also decide to think about your sexuality.

Thinking about it is important for your own and others' protection. You can review your knowledge of sexual anatomy, of sexually transmitted diseases or of pregnancy. Read books and talk to friends. It's okay to need support and reinforcement. If you want to, keep your own diary to aid your thinking and to record changes.

Integrating Sexuality And Identity

Because this part of adolescence is a more sophisticated version of Stage Four, the exercises and messages for working out a new identity remain the same. Use this short return to reintegrate the messages you already have learned.

Many people discover that they long ago converted "frightening" sexual feelings to "safe" nurturing ones. You can let yourself feel your sensory, sensual feelings. It's still okay to test power now that you're developing as a sexual person. Remember to take care of yourself, too. It is you who will face the consequences of pregnancy or venereal disease or hurt feelings. Use your power; have fun *and* cope with reality.

Integrating Sexuality With The Power Of Being Skillful

Becoming a sexually mature person requires developing a system of values and priorities. The foundation for these was created during Stage Five when we put together structures and roles related to our gender. We may need to reexamine these and update them. For example, women may need to reexamine messages such as:

- Be sexy but remain chaste.
- Be sophisticated but stay naive.
- Be smart enough to get a man and smart enough to keep him by hiding your intelligence.

Men may need to modify values such as:

- Play the field but don't let yourself get trapped.
- Be strong, stay cool, don't get involved and don't show feelings.
- Women are possessions that you must support and dominate.

Sex roles reinforce relationships that limit both partners because they structure actions and behavior according to gender instead of feelings, needs or natural abilities.

Contact with other people in the same stage is essential support for making sex role changes and replacing old values with new ones. Gender difference is not the determining factor. Regardless of gender, we each have the right to our own values and to develop our own abilities. Whether single or married, young or old, male or female, we can find ways to express ourselves.

Giving Affirmations And Support

There are many ways to give affirming messages; for example, Tania's friends affirmed her right to be a sexually mature person when they invited Tania and her lover over for dinner. Jack's father affirmed his right to be sexual and still have other needs when Jack brought his fiance home to meet the family and his father said, "You'll always be my son no matter how grown-up you get. If you need something you know you can ask me." Carrie's boyfriend's parents confirmed her right to succeed in the world when they taught her skills necessary for having a good job. "You don't have to settle on any old job," they said. "You're smart, you're deserving and you can find the kind of job you want."

On blank paper:

1. List the ways you like to affirm others who are in Stage Six.
2. Make a list of the things you like to do for and with others recycling Stage Six.

Finishing

Finishing Stage Six means saying goodbye to: (1) the child whom you once were, (2) this phase of your evolution and (3) friends whose lives will take them in different directions. The familiar structure of your daily life is dissolving into reunions, remembrances and memories preserved. In the same moment that you have gained the power to create your life anew and to create the human species anew, your childhood has passed with the demise of innocence. An unknown life awaits you that will test the powers you've developed. You will carry out new tasks, make great leaps of faith, show new capacities and discover new love. It is a major life passage.

As a grown-up, you still have needs and you can see that they are met. New opportunities are arising and you have the tools to work with. You've been through the cycle already. Some of this uncharted territory is actually going to be familiar terrain:

- This is the only time there is.
- The power is yours to claim.
- You have the right to be here.
- You have the power to act.
- You can think.
- You can know who you are.
- You can develop the skills you need.
- You can *go with love*.

You can make significant changes by actively using the affirming messages for Stage Six. If you're still having problems when you're using the affirmations and meeting your needs by doing the developmental tasks for Stage Six, you may need to work in another stage or you may need to work at a previous, younger age.

Exercises For
Developing The Power
Of Recycling

Taking Inventory

Reexamine and take inventory of your developmental stage by answering the following questions with yes or no.

_____ 1. Do you take enough time to just "be"?

_____ 2. Do you get the caring and affection you need from others?

_____ 3. Do you satisfy your sensory appetite with a variety of stimulation and environment?

_____ 4. Do you exercise your right to think for yourself and be independent?

_____ 5. Do you know who you are?

_____ 6. Are you free to develop the skills you want or need?

_____ 7. Are you satisifed with your sexuality?

_____ 8. Are you satisfied with your place in the world?

Now, compare the answers you have here to the answers you completed on the Developmental Script Questionnaire at the end of Chapter 2. Your script or fairy tale character will be blocked in certain issues more than others. These two sets of answers together can reveal connections between your present life limitations and past issues.

On separate paper answer these questions:

1. If you painted a picture of how you want your life to be, what would it look like? Use the vision you created in Chapter 1.
2. Now, what stands in the way?
3. What are the unresolved issues and developmental tasks you need to do?

Protection

Protection[45] is the experience of feeling safe enough to do what we need to do without unpleasant repercussions, such as fear of chastisement and abandonment, loss of love or further exposure to trauma or harm. We need protection to prevent trouble instead of having to fix a mess after it's been created. Some of the changes suggested in this book are safe to do in the company of willing friends and family. Other changes — those that require diving deep into primal layers of development should not be attempted without professional support and guidance.

You deserve the opportunity to have a satisfactory outcome in completing your developmental tasks. The purpose of this book in that regard has been twofold. First, it has acquainted you with your birthright as a human: your cycle of development and the stages within it. Second, it has provided tools to assess your strengths and weaknesses in the process along with some rudimentary supportive exercises.

Feelings of danger or hesitation are part of your protection. Trust them; they are a warning. Decide to continue exploring areas of growth where you feel intensely vulnerable and/or unsure, only when you feel secure that the people you are working with have the skills to see you through.

If you don't remember where the bathroom is, how to get out of bed or where you are, stop regressing without protection and find a therapeutic live-in arrangement until you can stay grown-up enough to handle daily life. If you can handle your daily life, but have many issues to resolve, you may want a regular schedule in which to work for a period of months. If you're fairly satisfied with your life, but have one issue you'd like to resolve, a short session or two may be sufficient.

There are many sources of support. Don't expect that everything you need will come from only one source. You don't have to limit yourself to working in only one situation or relationship.

Contracts: The Basis For Protection

A contract is a mutually understood agreement about responsibilities in relationships. Making a contract is a first step in creating a protective, problem-solving association. All relationships, including contractual ones, run into difficulties occasionally. By agreeing in advance to solve and not run away from these difficulties as they occur, both parties provide the safety necessary for carrying out developmental tasks. Whether the relationship is with a friend or therapist, contracts clarify what each person will do, how each will do it, what support is necessary and how each of you will know when the contract is completed.

To make a contract ask these questions:

- What is going on in your life that you want to change?
- When you change it, how will your life be different?
- What do you need to do to accomplish this?
- How will other people know when you've accomplished it?
- How long will you need to do it?
- How might you sabotage yourself?
- Will you agree not to sabotage yourself but instead to work on your urge to do so during a working session?

Contracts are inadequate if they are unclear and/or nonspecific, and if they lack straight talk or define an impossible task. Examples are saying, "I want to be happy" or "I want to earn more" (with no statement of what more is). Contracts that contain contradictory messages, such as stating, "I want to get along better with my wife and girlfriend" or ones that are open-ended and contain no stated goal are also inadequate and require modification.[46]

Guidelines For Maintaining Protection Within Contracts

We all have wisdom inherent in our developmental cycle. That means we're smart even if we don't have the IQ of a genius. When dealing with apparently self-defeating behavior, ask yourself:

1. "In what way is this really smart?" (Frame your answer within the context of your own developmental history. Go back stage by stage, using the answers to your Developmental Script Questionnaire until you find a developmental circumstance in which it makes sense.)
2. "What do I need to do to resolve it?"

The implications are that you do know somewhere inside what you need, that you can think and know what your needs are, that your needs are important and that you are expert when it comes to your own growth.

It's Your Script. You can change your life plan if you need to. Don't try to get rid of it by passing it on to somebody else like a hot potato.[47]

Maintain A Problem-Solving Position. If you're persecuting, rescuing or feeling victimized,[48] you're not in a problem-solving position. Use the affirming messages and ask for what you want.

Parenting, Mentoring and Therapeutic Contracts. When you need to finish developmental tasks from ages when you were young enough to need parents, you may want to make a corrective parenting contract with someone.[49] Or, you may want to establish a mentor relationship with a trusted guide. Do not attempt to get parenting or mentoring from someone if that person is not willing or if you don't have a contract with each other. Such situations only reinforce the fact that you can't get what you need. Instead, make a clear arrangement and be specific about the amount of time you need; such as the next five minutes, the next hour, the next month or the length of time you need to reach your goal.

Love and affection play a major role in the effectiveness of such relationships. When you feel genuinely cared for and acknowledged, you're more ready to make changes to develop your power. Learning to ask for or to give support is also easier in a loving atmosphere; otherwise you may feel too tied up and isolated to open up.

Relationships based on emotional involvement and personal intimacy are a potent healing force.

You may want the protection of private sessions, or of a group of people where you can be together in an open, trusting way, to work on developmental issues. Adequate leadership is essential in such groups. Investigate a potential situation carefully and avoid those that feel bad to you. Remember your sense of danger is still a good intuition to follow. Make sure the leaders are caring and good at what they do. The fact that someone has a degree or a license means little when dealing with these issues. You need somebody whose been there and who will stay with you and be responsive to what you need without taking over for you. Avoid groups where the motivation is profit, not people.

If this is your first exploration into therapy, you may want to ask leaders such questions as, "What qualifies you to do this work?" or "What have you done to solve *your* personal problems?" or "Will you work with me, and on what terms?" and "Do you think I need a different situation than this?"

Most good therapists are known by the work they do and the people whose lives they have helped change. Start listening to your friends. Ask around for the kinds of support you want to find. Feel free to make an initial interview appointment and then decide whether or not you want to work with a certain person. You have the right to be assertive and cautious. The kind of people you are looking for to work with will respect and support that.

In constructing your new developmental direction:

- Finish the old situation.
- Create a new, affirming message and use it.
- Make a new picture (a new scene).
- Make a new decision about how you want to act.
- Carry out the developmental tasks.
- Take time to integrate the new experiences.

CONCLUSION

Understanding grown-up life as a series of repeating stages has great significance for living. For example, it points the way to continue growing after childhood. As Roseanne put it, "Change and growth are not just a part of life, they are life itself. We're vital people as long as we're changing and tuned to our needs on a daily basis. Thinking of myself as 'already grown-up' *limits* my growth!"

Knowing adult life is based on stages that are basically predictable and familiar allows for self-knowledge, self-acceptance and basic security. We can know what our behavior patterns *are* so that we can open up and recognize who we are. As Marcia remarks, "I'm kinder and more empathetic to myself. I have the freedom to be me. I can make new choices in my life because I know I'm going to go through these stages to make the changes, and I can arrange for the support to do it."

Marcia's husband, Bill, (see Chapter 2 and Stage Two) added, "It helped me to open up to other options and avenues to pursue in life because these pathways were no longer blocked by yesterday's unfinished business. Also, understanding my stages helps me know when to move on because I recognize that feeling of completion at the end of them."

Fran offers, "What I do now in life and what I *can* do is influenced by the developmental tasks I've carried out. How — and even whether or not — I've carried out developmental sequences and finished them is knowledge that has helped me stop bugging myself, because reaching my goals becomes a matter of developing, not a matter of basic worth or okay-ness. I've also gained an increased tolerance level for other people. There's no sense expecting twelve-year-old behavior when the person's only six years old in that area."

Using affirming messages in her stages has been an important tool for Annette. She says, "Knowing myself in this way I also know other people because everybody's growth pattern is basically the same. Then I can knock down the barriers and increase the depth and closeness, the intimacy in my relationships."

Joe (see Stage Four) has used his knowledge to create, as he describes, ". . . a mutually supportive relationship within my family where we can learn and have fun together. We can get lost in the depth of an emotion and all of a sudden see the humor. We can laugh with someone about the situation and enjoy each other. We can be children."

Having been told how grown-up we're supposed to be, we may easily lose sight of how vital it is to go back to the beginning as a way of moving forward. Sometimes we need to recycle on primitive, stage-setting levels and not just on a current level. This has been significant to Sally, whom we met in Stage Four. She remarks, "Knowing this has increased my comfort level and helped me trust myself. I'd feel like a little girl and think there was something wrong with it. Or, I couldn't decide about something and think something was wrong with me. Now I realize that's me in one of the first two stages. I don't push myself because I know it won't last forever and it doesn't."

George realized doing developmental tasks can be a simple process with different stages. He admitted, "I found out you don't have to go through any crisis. It doesn't have to be painful or awful or scary or difficult. What's hard is fighting it by listening to cultural messages instead of your own developmental patterns. The more you understand your own recycling journey, the less pain and strain it will be."

We all have a right to be here, to move, to be active and to do things. We all have a right to be independent and think for ourselves to know who we are, to develop and practice our own expertise, to be sexual, to find our place in the world and to succeed.

Back to our own fundamental *Nature* is essential to our health and survival both as individuals and as a species. We need to sink our roots deep into the earth if we want to reach for the stars. Reading this book has been part of that process.

Things change, then come back to their beginnings. Like the circle of the sun and moon, the sky, the bodies of people and animals, the nests of birds, the days and seasons — all come back in a circle. The young grow old and from the old the young begin and grow. It is the Great Spirit's way.

Sacajawea[50]
Shoshoni Indian Guide
for Lewis and Clark Expedition

GLOSSARY

ADAPTED. A fixed pattern of imitating others instead of self-motivated behavior.

ADAPTIVE. The ability to size up a situation and act accordingly.

CONFRONT. To bring face to face.

CONTRACT. A legal, mutual agreement entered into between two or more competent parties stating each person's part; includes what will be exchanged.

CORRECTIVE PARENTING CONTRACT. An agreement entered into for the purpose of completing or aiding someone in completing tasks at childhood levels of development

CYCLE. A recurring period of time in which the processes, events and stages of life repeat.

CYCLE SABOTAGE. Interference with the normal course of development by needs that were unmet, by early decisions or unresolved traumas; or, the process of current development being undermined by these early, often unconscious influences.

DISCOUNT. To refuse to take into account; to devalue especially through not recognizing a person or a problem; to not acknowledge the problem's importance, the ability to solve it or the fact it can be solved.

ESCALATE. To increase the energy in a feeling or problem until it is all out of proportion.

EXCLUDING. A process of inviting parenting from others and also defending against it by making it not okay.

GAME. A series of ulterior transactions beginning with a discount, followed by a switch in roles and ending with a payoff that justifies having a problem rather than solving it.

GROUP. Several people organized into leadership and membership.

LIFE COURSE. The direction of an individual life over time or the pattern of specific events, relationships, achievements and aspirations.

LIFE CYCLE. The underlying and universal pattern denoting the revolution of time of an individual life, regardless of cultural patterns.

NEED. Something essential to the healthy life and growth of a person, such as "babies *need* touching" or "people *need* food and strokes". Also, what is necessary according to the stage of development.

OBSESSING. Controlling feelings or conflicts by continuous repetition of a thought.

PAYOFF. The purpose of game playing that switches responsibility for a feeling or problem.

PASSIVITY. To do nothing relevant to solving a problem.

PLAY GROUP. A group meeting arranged to support carrying out developmental tasks at specific (often younger) ages.

POWER. The ability to do or to act; also to cause to grow; the capacity for activity.

PROBLEM SOLVING. The process of finding solutions for problems or conflicts.

PROTECTION. Setting up situations to be safe, first by preventing trouble whenever possible and then by having effective ways of taking care of problems when they arise.

RACKET. A feeling or behavior used to cover another feeling, such as feeling scared and acting angry; used as emotional currency to extort attention.

RECYCLING. Nature's pattern of growth; one in which the sames stages of development that occurred during childhood are repeated throughout life.

SCRIPT. An unconscious life plan based on decisions made during childhood and reinforced by parents, like the written text of a play.

STAGE. A stable portion of the developmental cycle having its own needs, processes and distinctive characteristics. Also, a scene of action in the cycle of life; the platform upon which the primal theater of life is enacted.

STRAIGHT. Relating directly, without ulterior motives; in contrast to games.

STROKE. A unit of recognition such as a touch, a greeting or a kick.

STRUCTURE. Organized elements of experience constructed to serve as models for doing things.

SYMBOL. Something that stands for or represents another thing; an act or object representing an unconscious desire.

TESTING. Activity designed to establish independence; usually occurs in even numbered years of the cycle.

TRANSACTION. An exchange of strokes consisting of a stimulus from one person and a response from another.

TRANSACTIONAL ANALYSIS. A system of social psychiatry that provides methods for identifying what goes on between people; a form of psychotherapy; a complete theory of personality.

TRAUMA. A startling experience that has a lasting effect on mental life.

VISION. A vivid, imaginative conception of future life used to organize one's progress through the cyclic stages of life.

BIBLIOGRAPHY

Books

By Levin, Pamela

Les cycles de l'identite (French version of *Cycles of Power*). Paris, France: InterEditions, 1986.

How To Develop Your Personal Powers, A Workbook for Your Life's Time. Self-published, 1982.

Becoming The Way We Are (An Introduction To Personal Development and Recovery And In Life). 1974. Health Communications, 1988.

The Fuzzy Frequency (A Children's Book Illustrated by Sunny Mehler). 1978.

Credits

Bodmer, C. Annette. **The Gift Of Affirmations.** Savage, Minnesota: Affirmation Enterprises, 1985. (Based on Affirmations in *Becoming The Way We Are*, Levin, 1974.)

Lerner, Rockelle. **Daily Affirmations For Adult Children Of Alcoholics.** Florida: Health Communications, Inc., 1985. (Developmental Affirmations in this work based on *Becoming The Way We Are*, Levin, 1974.)

Clarke, Jean. **Self-Esteem: A Family Affair.** Minnesota: Winston Press, 1978. (Based on Developmental Theory in *Becoming The Way We Are*, Levin, 1974.)

Berne, MD, Eric. Contributed footnotes credited to E.W. (Emancipated Woman) in **Sex in Human Loving**, New York: Grove Press, 1970.

Publications

By Levin, Pamela

"The A/Mazing Journey." ITAA *Script* 15, no. 6 (Aug. 1985).

"The Cycle of Development." *Transactional Analysis Journal* 12, no. 2 (Apr. 1982).

"'A Developmental Script Questionnaire." *Transactional Analysis Journal* 2, no. 1 (Jan. 1981).

"We're Normally Not Neurotic." *Bulletin of the Eric Berne Seminar 1*, no. 2 (Jun. 1979): 15-17.

"Sex Roles, An Added Dimension to Script Theory." *Transactional Analysis Journal* (Translated into French for *Actualities En Analyse*) 2, no. 2 (1979).

"How We Develop Our Natural Child." *Bulletin of the Eric Berne Seminar* 1, no. 3 (Sept. 1979).

"Health Care Alternatives." A book review for ITAA *Script, 9*, no. 9 (Nov. 1979).

Une "Structuration de las Pensee." Pour se sentir bien plus vite *Actualities En Analyse Transactionnelle* 1, no. 1 (1978).

"The Development of Sex Role Scripting." Women's Issue of *Transactional Analysis Journal, 3,* no. 1 (Jan. 1977).

"Women's Oppression." *Transactional Analysis Journal* 7, no. 1 (Jan. 1977).

"Think Structure for Feeling Fine Faster." *Transactional Analysis Journal* 3, no. 1 (Jan. 1973). (Nominated for Eric Berne Scientific Award, 1976).

Co-author with Eric Berne, "Games Nurses Play." *American Journal of Nursing* (Mar. 1971). Reprinted in *Selected Readings for Clinical Nurses.*

By Others

About Development

Kendall, Jeni (Producer). **Birth and Beyond** (Film). Nimbin, NSW, Australia: North Country Flix.

Wilhelm/Baynes. **The I Ching** or **Book of Changes**. 3rd ed., Princeton, N.J.: Princeton University Press, 1950.

Rupertini, Alexander. **Cycles of Becoming.** Davis, Calif.: CRCS Publications, 1978.

Montague, Ashley. **Touching.** New York: Harper & Row, 1971.

Bridges, William. **The Seasons of Our Lives.** Rolling Hill Estate: Calif.: Wayfarer Press, 1977.

Gould, Roger. **Transformation, Growth and Change in Adult Life.** New York: Simon & Schuster, 1978.

Levinson, Daniel. **The Season of a Man's Life.** New York: Simon & Schuster, 1978.

Sheehey, Gail. **Passages, Predictable Crises of Adult Life.** New York: Dutton, 1976.

Weiss, Jonathan and Weiss, Laurie. "The Good Child Syndrome." from **TA: The State of the Art, a European Contribution.** Utrecht, The Netherlands: Foris Publications, 1984.

About Development And Parenting

Clarke, Jean. **Self Esteem: A Family Affair.** Minneapolis, Minn.: Winston Press, 1978.

Clarke, Jean. **Self Esteem: A Family Affair, Leaders Guide.** Minneapolis, Minn.: Winston Press, 1981.

About Regression

Schiff, Jacqui with Day, Beth. **All My Children.** New York: M. Evans & Co., 1970.

Rosenthal, Vic. "Holding: A Way Through the Looking Glass?" *Voices* (Spring, 1975).

Schiff, Jacqui and Schiff, Aaron. "Passivity." *Transactional Analysis Journal 1,* no. 1 (Jan. 1971).

Schiff, Jacqui, et al. **Cathexis Reader,** New York: Harper & Row, 1975.

Schiff, Jacqui. "Reparenting Schizophrenics." *Transactional Analysis Bulletin* 8, no. 31 (1969).

Lily, John. **The Center of the Cyclone.** New York: Julian Press, Inc., 1972.

About Cycles

Doczi, Gyorgy. **The Power of Limits.** Boston: Shambhala Publications, 1981.

Collin, Rodney. **The Theory of Celestial Influence.** New York: Samuel Weiser, 1974, 157-203.

Arguelles, Jose. **Earth Ascending.** Boston: Shambhala Publications, 1984.

Dewey, Edward R. **Cycles the Mysterious Forces that Trigger Events.** Hawthorne Books, 1971.

Rupertini, Alexander. **Cycles of Becoming, The Planetary Pattern of Growth,** Davis, Calif.: CRCS Publications, 1978.

Cycles (Bulletin of the Foundation for the Study of Cycles).

Purce, Jill. **The Mystic Spiral, A Journey of the Soul.** New York: Thames & Hudson, 1980.

People And Places

For a list of people and places that are resources for doing this work, write the author.

REFERENCES

1. Hilts, Philip. "The Clock Within." *Cycles* (Bulletin for the Study of Cycles) (Mar. 1982). (Reprinted by permission of *Science 81* Magazine, copyright of the American Association for the Advancement of Science.)

2. Berne, Eric. **Transactional Analysis in Psychotherapy.** New York: Grove Press, 1961, p. 23.

3. Berne, Eric. **What Do You Say After You Say Hello.** New York: Grove Press, 1971.

4. Berne, Eric. **Transactional Analysis in Psychotherapy.** New York: Grove Press, 1961, p. 17.

5. *Ibid.,* p. 125.

6. Montague, Ashley. **Growing Young.** New York: McGraw-Hill, 1982.

7. Buhler, Charlotte (ed.). **The Course of Human Life: The Study of Goals in the Humanistic Perspective.** New York: Springer Publishing Co., Inc., 1968.

8. Schaef, Anne Wilson. **Women's Reality.** Minneapolis, Minnesota: Winston Press, 1981.

9. Levin, Pamela. **Becoming The Way We Are.** 1st ed. rev., Berkeley: Self-published, 1974, pp. 11-12.

10. *Ibid.,* 2nd ed. rev.; Wenatchee, Washington: Directed Media, Inc., 1985, pp. 111-113.

11. Levin, Pam. "A Developmental Script Questionnaire." *Transactional Analysis Journal 2*, no. 1 (Jan. 1981): 77-80.

12. For how to use these messages when parenting children see: Bodmer, Annette. **The Gift of Affirmation.** (Affirmation Enterprises, P.O. Box 21, Savage, Minnesota 55378: Self-published, 1975) Clarke, Jean. **Self-Esteem: A Family Affair.** Minneapolis, Minnesota: Winston Press, 1978.

13. Levin, Pamela. **Becoming The Way We Are.** 1st ed., pp. 11-12.

14. Berne, Eric. **Games People Play,** New York: Grove Press, 1964.

15. Levin, Pamela. **Becoming The Way We Are**. 1st ed., p. 27.

16. The process of regression is described by: Schiff, Jacqui Lee with Day, Beth in **All My Children**. New York: M. Evans & Co., 1970.

17. Schiff, Jacqui and Schiff, Aaron. "Passivity." *Transactional Analysis Journal* 1, no. 1 (Jan. 1971).

18. Berne, Eric. **Games People Play**.

19. Levin, Pamela. **Becoming The Way We Are**. 1st ed., pp. 31-32.

20. Cass RN, Garcia and Cass, Paul. Pointed out the relationship of the stress mechanism to exploratory dynamics.

21. Berne, Eric. **Games People Play**.

22. Levin, Pamela. **Becoming The Way We Are**. 1st ed., pp. 35-36.

23. Schiff, Jacqui, et al. **Cathexis Readers**, New York: Harper & Row, 1975, p. 7.

24. Levin, Pamela. **Becoming The Way We Are**. 1st ed., pp. 37-42.

25. Berne, Eric. **Games People Play**.

26. Levin, Pamela. **Becoming The Way We Are**. 1st ed., p. 41.

27. Crossman, Patricia. Clarification and interpretation of Stage Four dynamics was accomplished in a series of interviews, 1977-1978.

28. Levin, Pamela. **Becoming The Way We Are**. 1st ed., pp. 37-42.

29. Berne, Eric. **Games People Play**.

30. Levin, Pamela. **Becoming The Way We Are**. 1st ed., p. 47.

31. *Ibid.*, pp. 37-42.

32. Berne, Eric. **Games People Play**.

33. Steiner, Claude. "A Script Checklist." *Transactional Analysis Bulletin* 6, (Apr. 1967): 110-114.

34. Levin, Pamela. "Think Structure for Feeling Fine Faster." *Transactional Analysis Journal* 3, no. 1 (Jan. 1973).

35. Clarke, J. I. Affirmation Structure, Personal communication, 1980.

36. For additional methods, see Bodmer, C. Annette, **The Gift of Affirmation**, Affirmation Enterprises, P.O. Box 21, Savage, MN 55378, 1985.

37. This list was developed by members of Mothers, Fathers and Others Who Care About Children, Minneapolis, Minnesota.

38. The therapeutic effectiveness of holding is discussed by Rosenthal, Vic in "Holding: A Way Through the Looking Glass?" *Voices* (Spring 1975) pp. 2-7.

39. Establishing Boundaries exercise designed by Dierks, Sally, Hartmann, Sheila and Clarke, Jean. Mothers, Fathers and Others Community, Minneapolis, Minnesota.

40. Confrontation Guidelines by Schiff, Aaron Wolfe in a lecture demonstration, International Transactional Analysis Association, Summer Conference, 1973.

41. Recipes contributed by Freund, Claudia, Mothers, Fathers and Others Community, Minneapolis, Minnesota.

42. This exercise, used in many personal growth trainings, was conveyed through personal communication with Clarke, J. I., 1980.

43. Levin, Pamela. "Sex Roles: An Added Dimension to Script Theory." *Transactional Analysis Journal* 2, no. 2, 1979.

44. Many of the methods of supporting grown-ups being eight years old were developed by Hilliker, Virginia.

45. Crossman, Patricia. "Permission Protection and Potency." *Transactional Analysis Bulletin* 5, no. 19 (Jul. 1966): 152-154.

46. Vanderburgh, Jan. "Inadequacy Contracts and How to Avoid Them." Unpublished monograph, Littleton, Colorado, 1975.

47. English, Fanita. "Episcript and the Hot Potato Game." *Transactional Analysis Journal* 8, no. 33 (1969).

48. Karpman, Stephen. "Fairy Tales and Script Drama Analysis." *Transactional Analysis Journal* 7, no. 26 (Apr. 1968).

49. Schiff, Jacqui. "Reparenting Schizophrenics." *Transactional Analysis Bulletin* 8, no. 31 (1969): 47-63.

50. Waldo, Anna Lee. **Sacajawea**. New York: Avon Books, 1978, p. 1301.

Other Books By . . .

HEALTH COMMUNICATIONS, INC.

Enterprise Center
3201 Southwest 15th Street
Deerfield Beach, FL 33442
Phone: 800-851-9100

ADULT CHILDREN OF ALCOHOLICS
Janet Woititz
Over a year on The New York Times Best Seller list,this book is the primer
on Adult Children of Alcoholics.
ISBN 0-932194-15-X $6.95

STRUGGLE FOR INTIMACY
Janet Woititz
Another best seller, this book gives insightful advice on learning to love
more fully.
ISBN 0-932194-25-7 $6.95

DAILY AFFIRMATIONS: For Adult Children of Alcoholics
Rokelle Lerner
These positive affirmations for every day of the year paint a mental picture
of your life as you choose it to be.
ISBN 0-932194-27-3 $6.95

*CHOICEMAKING: For Co-dependents, Adult Children and Spirituality
Seekers* — Sharon Wegscheider-Cruse
This useful book defines the problems and solves them in a positive way.
ISBN 0-932194-26-5 $9.95

LEARNING TO LOVE YOURSELF: Finding Your Self-Worth
Sharon Wegscheider-Cruse
"Self-worth is a choice, not a birthright", says the author as she shows us
how we can choose positive self-esteem.
ISBN 0-932194-39-7 $7.95

LET GO AND GROW: Recovery for Adult Children
Robert Ackerman
An in-depth study of the different characteristics of adult children of
alcoholics with guidelines for recovery.
ISBN 0-932194-51-6 $8.95

LOST IN THE SHUFFLE: The Co-dependent Reality
Robert Subby
A look at the unreal rules the co-dependent lives by and the way out of the
dis-eased reality.
ISBN 0-932194-45-1 $8.95

New Books . . .
from Health Communications

BRADSHAW ON: THE FAMILY: A Revolutionary Way of Self-Discovery
John Bradshaw
The host of the nationally televised series of the same name shows us how families can be healed and we as individuals can realize our full potential.
ISBN 0-932194-54-0 $9.95

HEALING THE CHILD WITHIN: Discovery and recovery for Adult Children of Dysfunctional Families — Charles Whitfield
Dr. Whitfield defines, describes and discovers how we can reach our Child Within to heal and nurture our woundedness.
ISBN 0-932194-40-0 $8.95

WHISKY'S SONG: An Explicit Story of Surviving in an Alcoholic Home
Mitzi Chandler
A beautiful but brutal story of growing up where violence and neglect are everyday occurrences conveys a positive message of survival and love.
ISBN 0-932194-42-7 $6.95

New Books on Spiritual Recovery . . .
from Health Communications

THE JOURNEY WITHIN: A Spiritual Path to Recovery
Ruth Fishel
This book will lead you from your dysfunctional beginnings to the place within where renewal occurs.
ISBN 0-932194-41-9 $8.95

LEARNING TO LIVE IN THE NOW: 6-Week Personal Plan To Recovery
Ruth Fishel
The author gently introduces you to the valuable healing tools of meditation, positive creative visualization and affirmations.
ISBN 0-932194-62-1 $7.95

GENESIS: Spirituality in Recovery for Co-dependents
by Julie D. Bowden and Herbert L. Gravitz
A self-help spiritual program for adult children of trauma, an in-depth look at "turning it over" and "letting go".
ISBN 0-932194-56-7 $6.95

GIFTS FOR PERSONAL GROWTH AND RECOVERY
Wayne Kritsberg
Gifts for healing which include journal writing, breathing, positioning and meditation.
ISBN 0-932194-60-5 $6.95

Books from . . .
Health Communications

THIRTY-TWO ELEPHANT REMINDERS: A Book of Healthy Rules
Mary M. McKee
Concise advice by 32 wise elephants whose wit and good humor will also
be appearing in a 12-step calendar and greeting cards.
ISBN 0-932194-59-1 $3.95

BREAKING THE CYCLE OF ADDICTION: For Adult Children of Alcoholics
Patricia O'Gorman and Philip Oliver-Diaz
For parents who were raised in addicted families, this guide teaches you
about Breaking the Cycle of Addiction from *your* parents to your children.
Must reading for any parent.
ISBN 0-932194-37-0 $8.95

AFTER THE TEARS: Reclaiming The Personal Losses of Childhood
Jane Middelton-Moz and Lorie Dwinnel
Your lost childhood must be grieved in order for you to recapture your
self-worth and enjoyment of life. This book will show you how.
ISBN 0-932194-36-2 $7.95

ADULT CHILDREN OF ALCOHOLICS SYNDROME: From Discovery to Recovery
Wayne Kritsberg
Through the Family Integration System and foundations for healing the
wounds of an alcoholic-influenced childhood are laid in this important
book.
ISBN 0-932194-30-3 $7.95

OTHERWISE PERFECT: People and Their Problems with Weight
Mary S. Stuart and Lynnzy Orr
This book deals with all the varieties of eating disorders, from anorexia to
obesity, and how to cope sensibly and successfully.
ISBN 0-932194-57-5 $7.95

Orders must be prepaid by check, money order, MasterCard or Visa.
Purchase orders from agencies accepted (attach P.O. documentation)
for billing. Net 30 days.
    Minimum shipping/handling — $1.25 for orders less than $25. For
orders over $25, add 5% of total for shipping and handling. Florida
residents add 5% sales tax.